PRAYING THE ATTRIBUTES OF GOD

PRAYING

the

ATTRIBUTES

of

GOD

a daily guide to EXPERIENCING
HIS GREATNESS

ANN
SPANGLER

Bestselling author of *Praying the Names of God*

Tyndale House Publishers, Inc.
Carol Stream, Illinois

Visit Tyndale online at www.tyndale.com.

TYNDALE and Tyndale's quill logo are registered trademarks of Tyndale House Publishers, Inc.

Praying the Attributes of God: A Daily Guide to Experiencing His Greatness

Designed by Jacqueline L. Nuñez

Edited by Stephanie Rische

Published in association with Yates & Yates (www.yates2.com).

Library of Congress Cataloging-in-Publication Data

Spangler, Ann.
 Praying the attributes of God : a daily guide to experiencing his greatness / Ann Spangler.
   pages cm
 Includes bibliographical references.
 ISBN 978-1-4143-3598-8
 1. God (Christianity)—Attributes—Prayers and devotions. I. Title.
 BT130.S63 2013
 231′.4—dc23   2013011352

Printed in the United States of America

19	18	17	16	15	14	13
7	6	5	4	3	2	1

Contents

A Crash Course on God *vii*

Chapter 1   God Cares about You   *1*
Loving

Chapter 2   God Is Better than You Think   *21*
Good

Chapter 3   God Is Bigger than You Think   *39*
Infinite

Chapter 4   God Is Not Moody   *57*
Unchangeable, Immutable

Chapter 5   God Is Not Weak   *75*
All Powerful, Omnipotent

Chapter 6   God Is Close to Everywhere   *91*
Present Everywhere, Omnipresent

Chapter 7   God Is Never Surprised   *107*
All Knowing, Omniscient

Chapter 8   God Is Never Frustrated   *125*
Patient

Chapter 9   God Always Knows What to Do   *141*
Wise

Chapter 10   God Has No Limits   *161*
Eternal, Self-Sufficient

Chapter 11   God Is a Lover   *179*
Jealous

Chapter 12 God Is Always Fair   195
            Just, Righteous
Chapter 13 God Leans toward Compassion   213
            Merciful
Chapter 14 God Never Gives Up   231
            Faithful
Chapter 15 God Is Better than Anyone You Know   249
            Holy
Chapter 16 God Is an Artist   265
            Creative
Chapter 17 God Is above It All   285
            Transcendent

            Acknowledgments *301*
            Notes *303*
            About the Author *307*

A CRASH COURSE ON GOD

Why It's Good to Learn about His Attributes

I long for God, not the works of God.
Clement of Alexandria

Imagine never being able to distinguish music from noise. Every song, every symphony, every note would sound garbled and unpleasant. You'd struggle to stifle your laughter when you saw friends making fools of themselves belting out the words to their favorite songs or gyrating across the dance floor to a melody you couldn't detect. And what about all the money spent downloading music or the time wasted listening to a bunch of disagreeable sounds strung together? Wouldn't it all seem rather bizarre?

That was Austin Chapman's perspective for nearly twenty-three years. Born deaf, Austin was at peace with his situation. "All music," he explains, "sounded like trash through my hearing aids." But that changed the day he tried on a new pair capable of distributing higher frequencies with greater clarity.

Suddenly the young filmmaker heard sounds he didn't even know existed—the scraping of his shoe on carpet, the clicking of a computer keyboard, the whir of a fan. That night, friends decided to give him a crash course on music. He listened in amazement to Mozart, Elvis, Michael Jackson, and more.

"When Mozart's 'Lacrimosa' came on," Chapman says, "I was blown away by the beauty of it. At one point of the song, it sounded like angels singing and I suddenly realized that this was the first time I was able to appreciate music. Tears rolled down my face and I tried to hide it. . . . I finally understood the power of music."[1]

Chapman's story reminds me of my first experience with God. Before that, most of what I'd heard about him sounded garbled and boring, a bit like trash coming through hearing aids. These bits of knowledge didn't move me; instead, they left me feeling cold and a bit fearful. What little faith I had vanished shortly after I entered college. I did my best to make peace with my god- less state as though it were completely natural, the only rational response to life.

But then God disarmed me. He surprised me by being real, by helping me see that the god I had rejected didn't even exist. In truth, I hadn't discarded God, but only a caricature formed by my own and others' misperceptions. When the real God showed up, he changed my life. He upended my world. He blew my mind.

And he keeps doing it—surprising me, catching me off guard, shattering my false images of him. And that is true for most of us as we live out the Christian life. In our sanest moments, we realize that the most important thing we can do is to pursue God; to hound him, even; to prayerfully insist that he give us a clearer revelation of who he is, because by doing so, we are fulfilling the purpose for which he made us. It is in his presence that life and joy are to be found. All other things, the things that clamor for our worship and insist on our undivided attention, are revealed for what they are—beautiful trifles, which when compared to God seem merely like tinfoil reflections of his glory.

The Old Testament prophets knew about our susceptibility to

idols and to phony worship. Over and over they railed against idolatry, linking it to blindness. Listen to Isaiah describing those who worship idols:

> Such stupidity and ignorance!
>> Their eyes are closed, and they cannot see.
>> Their minds are shut, and they cannot think.
> The person who made the idol never stops to reflect,
>> "Why, it's just a block of wood!
> I burned half of it for heat
>> and used it to bake my bread and roast my meat.
> How can the rest of it be a god?
>> Should I bow down to worship a piece of wood?"
> The poor, deluded fool feeds on ashes.
>> He trusts something that can't help him at all.
> Yet he cannot bring himself to ask,
>> "Is this idol that I'm holding in my hand a lie?"
>
> ISAIAH 44:18-20

Indeed, throughout Scripture, we see this link between God's judgment and the dulling of our human senses.[2] Jesus, the one famous for opening the eyes of the blind and the ears of the deaf, makes this link crystal clear:

"I entered this world to render judgment—to give sight to the blind and to show those who think they see that they are blind."

Some Pharisees who were standing nearby heard him and asked, "Are you saying we're blind?"

"If you were blind, you wouldn't be guilty," Jesus replied. "But you remain guilty because you claim you can see."

> JOHN 9:39-41

If we want to see God more clearly, we have to be willing to let go of false images when we are given the grace to recognize them for what they are. Human vision, of course, is always impaired. Our deluded hearts mislead us. We see only to the extent that God graciously opens our eyes—the eyes of the blind.

Not long ago, while I was puzzling over the difficulties that bear down hard upon our lives—things like job loss, illness, financial pressure, relational conflict, and other maladies, it occurred to me that the emotional pain we feel as a result of our troubles is often magnified by a colossal misunderstanding—one common to the human race. This misunderstanding arises from our lack of vision. Most of the time, we don't clearly see ourselves or our circumstances or the God we love. As Paul says, we are always looking "through a glass, darkly" (1 Corinthians 13:12, KJV). So our vision is to some extent blurred, limited, and confused, putting us into the foreground while everything else recedes to the background. Our fears, our aspirations, our troubles—these are the focal points that command our attention.

This pattern of distortion happens to everyone, Christians and non-Christians alike, even though God has revealed truths about himself that should untangle and upend our twisted views of what is really going on. Despite the fact that we now see God in the picture, we Christians, still plagued by selfishness and fear, often relegate him to the blurry background.

When I was a child, I was introduced to a god who was all seeing, all powerful, and all knowing. But to my child's mind, he looked distant, fearful, and untrustworthy. How can you feel close to a god who holds you in disdain for your many failures, a perfect god whom your flawed self is incapable of pleasing? Fortunately, that imbalanced and distorted vision of God eventually gave way to the understanding that God loved me like the most faithful of fathers—indeed, that he had given his Son to save me and take away my sins.

In the years that followed my conversion, I watched as the church jettisoned the hard god of my youth in favor of a much softer god—one who is always tender and tolerant and who does not demand too much of his people. In the Western church, notions of God's holiness and awe have receded to the background or have disappeared altogether. But that soft god produces only soft followers, spiritually enfeebled and vulnerable to the shaping power of the surrounding culture and to the ever-changing circumstances that characterize human life.

What am I arguing for? A return to the hard god? By no means. Let's not discard one distortion so we can embrace another. What we need is something only God can give—a true and deeper vision of who he is as the almighty, everlasting God, who is holy and yet merciful, jealous and yet loving, righteous and yet forgiving. This is the God of Abraham and Sarah and Moses and David and Mary Magdalene and Peter and John and all the faithful who have preceded us. They lived with a sense of God's majesty, a life-shaping knowledge of his greatness and goodness. As A. W. Tozer has said, "The great Church has for centuries lived on the character of God. She's preached God, she's prayed to God, she's declared God, she's honored God, she's elevated God, she's witnessed to God."[3]

Let us not settle, then, for a vision of God that is thin and anemic, one that will fall to pieces when life becomes more difficult than we can bear. Instead, let us pray that God will draw us out of our complacency so that we might hunger and thirst for more of him.

Studying God

One way to increase our yearning for God is to approach him both prayerfully and humbly through study. In Jewish tradition, study undertaken in this way is the highest form of worship.

But how can we possibly study a being who is vastly superior to anything or anyone we've ever encountered? Perhaps one way to begin is by resurrecting an old-fashioned word. The word is *attribute* (a-truh-byoot). God's attributes are facets of his character revealed in the Bible. Some might object that it is impossible for human beings to comprehend God—and they would be right. But God can enable us to experience him in deeper ways as we learn more about him. Why else would he reveal himself if he did not want to be known?

While studying his attributes, we must resurrect other old-fashioned words such as *holiness, omnipotence, omniscience, omnipresence, righteousness, sovereignty,* and *transcendence.* (Are you snoring yet?) But rather than boring us to death, these words, when excavated for their biblical meanings, may end up thrilling us and freeing us from the colossal mistake of concluding that God is too weak or too removed or too soft to enable us to live with joy and fearlessness regardless of the problems we face. Who knows—a thoroughgoing study of the attributes of God may even show us that God is far bigger and far better than we think. Like music heard clearly for the first time, our prayerful study of God may yield a depth of experience that amazes and delights us, putting God where he belongs—in the foreground—as our cares and concerns recede to the background.

Perhaps what we need most is not a crash course in music but a crash course in God. As we immerse ourselves in God's self-revelation, found within the pages of the Bible, we need to pray that his Spirit will show us who he really is. Studying the Bible without the guidance of the Holy Spirit will not yield the longed-for results.

One caveat: even with the best of intentions, it is easy to misunderstand the God we seek. Part of the problem is that sin clouds our vision, distorts our view. We want a god we can control, one we can manage and use. But God won't be reduced by our selfish aspirations. Another hindrance is our own limited capacity. We are like children trying to scoop the ocean into a bucket—finite beings trying to comprehend the mind and heart of an infinite God.

At times we doubt God—perhaps not outwardly, but secretly. We judge his motives, particularly when things go wrong, suspecting him of being unkind, unfeeling, or even cruel. He doesn't act the way we think he should or according to our timelines. Or he fails to act at all. We pray and pray and hear no answer. Only silence.

Our judgments, based as they are on faulty and inadequate knowledge, can lead to feelings of disappointment, hurt, anger, and confusion. *How, we wonder, can a good God tolerate the cruelty and violence that often characterize our world?* Because we don't understand, we begin to question God's motives, his power, and his goodness. We wonder how an all-powerful God has not yet managed to clean up the universe. Though Christianity has had two thousand years to spread, and though it has made enormous contributions to the world, there is still so much darkness.

Catherine the Great was one of the world's most powerful rulers in the second half of the eighteenth century. Reigning from 1762 until her death in 1796, Catherine longed to bring Russian culture and government in line with the Enlightenment principles of Western Europe. But it was a daunting task. Here's how she replied to Diderot, a French philosopher who pressed her to transform Russia along more enlightened lines:

> I have listened with the greatest pleasure to all the
> inspirations of your brilliant mind. But all your grand
> principles, which I understand very well, would do
> splendidly in books and very badly in practice. In
> your plans for reform, you are forgetting the difference

between our two positions: you work only on paper
which accepts anything, is smooth and flexible and
offers no obstacles either to your imagination or your
pen, while I, poor empress, work on human skin,
which is far more sensitive and touchy.[4]

Reading Catherine's response reminded me that God has
deliberately chosen to work through a rather intransigent
medium—the medium of human skin. As Catherine so archly
observed, this is a medium that is "sensitive and touchy." It does
not quickly yield to abstract solutions, sound as they might be.
Because God is working in and through broken people whose
souls are neither smooth nor flexible, his activity may seem
obscured and obstructed at times. He doesn't "live up to" our
idealistic notions of how he should act or what he should do.
As Paul says, we see, but through a glass darkly. Despite our
confusion and obvious limitations, God has revealed himself in
Scripture, and he has filled us with his Spirit so we can begin to
understand more about who he is.

One thing to keep in mind when it comes to God is that an
attribute is an artificial construct, a helpful way to learn about
God. But God cannot be divided into his various attributes, nor
will he act in ways that contradict himself. He is still just, for
instance, even when he is expressing his mercy, and still loving
when expressing his jealousy.

As A. W. Tozer points out, "God's attributes are not isolated
traits of His character but facets of His unitary being. They are
not things-in-themselves; they are, rather, thoughts by which
we think of God, aspects of a perfect whole, names given to
whatever we know to be true of the Godhead. To have a correct
understanding of the attributes it is necessary that we see them
all as one. We can think of them separately but they cannot be
separated."[5]

How to Use This Book

In the pages that follow, we will delve into the Bible in order to explore the attributes of God—aspects of his character that are clearly revealed. To help you reflect on one attribute each week, I have developed a devotional program intended to lead you to greater understanding and deeper prayer. Each week's readings contain five main elements: background information, Bible study, devotions, Bible promises, and prayer. Here's how a week unfolds:

Monday: A key Scripture passage that reveals a particular attribute of God, as well as background information and a brief Bible study to help you understand this attribute.

Tuesday, Wednesday, and Thursday: Devotions to help you pray specific Scripture passages that relate to the attribute you are learning about. These are designed to provide a springboard for personal prayer and praise.

Friday: A reflection that helps you see how this attribute connects to God's promises in Scripture. It offers key Bible passages that can be read, reflected on, or even memorized. A section entitled "Continued Prayer and Praise" lists additional passages related to the attribute that can be prayed and studied over the weekend for those who desire to do so.

As you read through this book, I hope you will share my sense that learning more about God's attributes is like drawing water from a deep well—the kind that can refresh and invigorate your faith. In the days and weeks ahead, may God give you the boldness to prayerfully insist that he nourish, sustain, and strengthen you with a clearer revelation of who he is.

The nineteenth-century preacher Charles Spurgeon once remarked, "No subject of contemplation will tend more to humble the mind, than thoughts of God. . . . But while the subject humbles the mind it also expands it."[6] May God reward your efforts with a deeper sense of how big he is so you may live your life wide open to all the opportunities that come to those who know how great God is.

1

GOD CARES
ABOUT YOU

LOVING

His Nature

From a natural standpoint, the most surprising thing about God is that he is love. It is not hard to conceive of a divine being who possesses immeasurable power or immortality or knowledge—other religions have such gods. For some of us, it is not that difficult to envision a god who expresses affection for us. But who could have dreamed up a being whose love is so extreme that he became incarnate to prove it? On the face of things, God would seem like a bad negotiator—trading power for weakness, riches for poverty, honor for humiliation. He even traded light for darkness, spending nine months in the womb so that he could convince us of his love and reconcile us to himself. God's love is extreme and fierce. He is a suitor who won't be put off, won't be denied, won't be spurned—unless, of course, we are obstinate and foolish enough to believe that he really doesn't love us despite the obvious proofs of his love. For those who will receive him, his love is unfailing, steadfast, eternal, full of kindness, and far beyond anything we could ever ask or imagine.

Key Scripture

This is how God loved the world: He gave his one and only Son, so that everyone who believes in him will not perish but have eternal life. God sent his Son into the world not to judge the world, but to save the world through him.

JOHN 3:16-17

Monday

GOD REVEALS HIMSELF

This is how God loved the world: He gave his one and only Son, so that everyone who believes in him will not perish but have eternal life. God sent his Son into the world not to judge the world, but to save the world through him.

JOHN 3:16-17

What shall we say about such wonderful things as these? If God is for us, who can ever be against us? Since he did not spare even his own Son but gave him up for us all, won't he also give us everything else? Who dares accuse us whom God has chosen for his own? No one—for God himself has given us right standing with himself. Who then will condemn us? No one—for Christ Jesus died for us and was raised to life for us, and he is sitting in the place of honor at God's right hand, pleading for us.

Can anything ever separate us from Christ's love? Does it mean he no longer loves us if we have trouble or calamity, or are persecuted, or hungry, or destitute, or in danger, or threatened with death? (As the Scriptures say, "For your sake we are killed every day; we are being slaughtered like sheep.") No, despite all these things, overwhelming victory is ours through Christ, who loved us.

And I am convinced that nothing can ever separate us from God's love. Neither death nor life, neither angels nor demons, neither our fears for today nor our worries about tomorrow—not even the powers of hell can separate us from God's love. No power in the sky above or in the earth below—indeed, nothing in all creation will ever be able to separate us from the love of God that is revealed in Christ Jesus our Lord.

ROMANS 8:31-39

Understanding His Love

The Bible uses two primary images to speak to us of God's love. In the Hebrew Scriptures (the Old Testament), his love is portrayed through the metaphor of marital love and commitment. He is a loving God who justly demands, though does not get, absolute fidelity from the people he loves. Even so, he continues to love them despite their unfaithfulness. The book of Hosea speaks of God binding himself to his people forever. The New Testament extends this metaphor by identifying Jesus as the Bridegroom and the church as his bride.

Scripture also uses the metaphor of parental love. Throughout the Old Testament, God is described as a loving Father to his people, Israel. Jesus develops this imagery in a way that shocks his contemporaries—addressing God as his Father and inviting his followers to do the same.

The Hebrew word *'ahab* can be translated "love, lovers, friends, allies." It refers to the love between husband and wife, as well as to the love that exists between parents and children. It can also refer to the intimate bond of friendship. Used thirty-two times throughout Scripture in connection with God, it speaks of his faithful love for Israel and his love for justice and righteousness.

Deuteronomy 6:5 commands God's people to "love the LORD your God with all your heart, all your soul, and all your strength." This Scripture has become part of a larger prayer called the *Shema*, the first words of which are drawn from this passage: "Hear, O Israel: The LORD our God, the LORD is one" (Deuteronomy 6:4, NIV). Observant Jews recite this prayer morning and evening, and often on their deathbeds, expressing their heartfelt response to God's faithful love.

Biblical love is not merely a matter of affectionate feelings or passion but is expressed through loving actions. Just as God shows his faithful love by acting redemptively in the lives of his people, we are called to show our love for God through obeying him, loving his Word, and living in faithfulness.

The other Old Testament word for love is *hesed*, which can be translated "mercy, loving-kindness, covenant faithfulness." It speaks richly of the undeserved love given by someone who is in a position of power, thereby capturing the generosity of God's love.

In the New Testament, the verb *agapaō* and the noun *agapē* are used to describe human love as well as the love God has for people. This love is completely undeserved, stemming from God's character rather than from anything in us that would attract his love. The New Testament also uses the Greek verb *phileō* to speak both of human and divine love and often to describe the love between friends.

If we have any doubts about the fierce nature of God's love, we have only to remember the words of John 3:16: "This is how God loved the world: He gave his one and only Son, so that everyone who believes in him will not perish but have eternal life."

Such sacrificial love demands a response. Like Jesus did, we are called to love our enemies. This doesn't mean we have to feel affection for them, but it does mean we must act in love toward them. Galatians 5:22 describes love as a fruit of the Spirit. Only God's Spirit alive within us can enable us to receive God's love and express it to others.

When we love God, we cannot help but love our neighbors.

Lord, no one has loved me the way you have. Even when I was far from you, you called me and fought for me and stretched out your arm to save me. Thank you for blessing me every day—for speaking to me, sustaining me, forgiving me, refusing to give up on me. Thank you for protecting my soul. I love you, Lord.

Studying His Love

1. What comes to mind when you hear the word *love*? How does your experience of love compare with the biblical ideal?
2. What in your life makes you doubt God's love?
3. What do you think it means to love God with "all your heart, all your soul, and all your strength"? Be specific.
4. How have you been able to express the love of God to others?
5. How would your life be different if you could affirm Paul's words from Romans 8:31-32 in every situation, saying, "If God is for me, who can ever be against me? Since he did not spare even his own Son but gave him up for me, won't he also give me everything else?"
6. Take a moment to pray, asking God to deepen your knowledge of his unfailing love so you can reflect his kindness to others.

Tuesday

PRAYING IN LIGHT OF GOD'S LOVE

This is how God loved the world: He gave his one and only Son, so that everyone who believes in him will not perish but have eternal life.

JOHN 3:16

Reflect On: John 3:16
Praise God: For Jesus, the irrefutable proof of God's love
Offer Thanks: Because God will never stop loving you
Confess: Any tendency to doubt God's love
Ask God: To help you perceive the depth of his love for
                you and for others

Not long ago I was swimming laps in a pool near my home. Normally my goggles help me to see the line down the center of the lane so I don't incur brain damage by swimming straight into the side of the pool. That day my progress was particularly slow because the goggles kept filling with water. About halfway through, after stopping every half lap to adjust them, I identified the problem. It seems I had put the goggles on upside down. No wonder they were taking on water.

Afterward, it occurred to me that upside-down goggles could be a useful metaphor for describing an affliction many of us share. When it comes to understanding God's love, some of us have things upside down. Though we've heard that God is love, and though we can believe he loves others, we can't quite believe he loves us. So we try hard to be good, and we wallow in guilt whenever we fail to measure up. We try to exercise faith but find it difficult because we lack the energy that comes from knowing we are loved.

Part of the problem is that we live in a fallen world. Many of us have never experienced unconditional love. Always there have been strings attached.

A second problem is that there is demonic interference. Like static on a radio, this interference takes the form of doubts and lies that the devil tries to implant so that it will become impossible for us to perceive how much God cares about us. If he can damage our confidence in God's character, he can impede or even destroy our Christian witness.

Suffering can also sharpen our doubts. *How, we wonder, could a powerful, all-loving God allow evil into our lives? If he is a loving Father, why doesn't he do a better job of protecting us?*

The answer to such questions is not simple. It comes in part from knowing God more deeply so we can understand the interplay between love and freedom. It also comes from comprehending that real love is multifaceted and stronger than mere affection.

As we learn more about God's attributes, we may find that we are able to turn our spiritual goggles right side up so we can perceive his love more clearly, interpreting life's events not in terms of our circumstances but in light of the truth we know: "This is how God loved the world: He gave his one and only Son, so that everyone who believes in him will not perish but have eternal life" (John 3:16).

Wednesday

PRAYING IN LIGHT OF GOD'S LOVE

When we were utterly helpless, Christ came at just the right time and died for us sinners. Now, most people would not be willing to die for an upright person, though someone might perhaps be willing to die for a person who is especially good. But God showed his great love for us by sending Christ to die for us while we were still sinners.

ROMANS 5:6-8

"Teacher, which is the most important commandment in the law of Moses?"

Jesus replied, "'You must love the LORD *your God with all your heart, all your soul, and all your mind.' This is the first and greatest commandment. A second is equally important: 'Love your neighbor as yourself.' The entire law and all the demands of the prophets are based on these two commandments."*

MATTHEW 22:36-40

Reflect On: Romans 5:6-8; Matthew 22:36-40
Praise God: For being love
Offer Thanks: Because God first loved you
Confess: Any tendency to think you have to earn
                God's love
Ask God: To let his love overflow in you

⌒

I have a friend whose teenage son has difficulty showing any kind of affection. The other day his younger sister asked whether he loved her. Chase just shrugged as if to say, *Maybe I do, maybe I don't, probably not, but who cares?* But his little sister wouldn't give up. She proceeded to ask a long line of questions: "Who do you love? How about your favorite teacher at school? What about the dog?" Chase couldn't work up much enthusiasm for anyone except the dog.

Then came the question my friend couldn't help but overhear: "Chase, do you love Mom and Dad?"

"Kind of," Chase replied, his voice flat.

Though it wasn't what my friend wanted to hear, she wasn't surprised. While many teenagers fail the "love test," her son had never been good at it. She knew that her autistic son had difficulty expressing love for anyone. I wondered about the impact this must have had on their relationship. We parents can put up with a lot because we know that deep down our children love us. But what would it be like to care for a child who seems incapable of reciprocating, when love only moves in one direction?

When we think about love, we often think about people who are attractive to us. We love them because they're beautiful, kind, affectionate, caring, courageous, smart, funny, or good. Something about them stirs our affection. But God is different. His love isn't fixed on us because we're good looking or great or perfect. The impetus for his love lies entirely within himself. The Bible says that God loved us when we were still wretched, still off track, still living in a way that deeply offended him. No law of mutual attraction was at work. God loved us simply because at his core *he is love*. That's why Jesus could say to his followers that if someone slapped them on the cheek, they should turn the other cheek for another slap. He was talking about loving unlovely people with divine love, not human love.

Many of us are still applying a human model to our relationship with God. Perhaps that's why we find it so difficult to believe God loves us. We think we're the ones who need to become lovable. Certain that we don't deserve God's love, we perpetually doubt him.

Isn't it time to stop making that mistake—to turn to God once and for all, surrendering our sin and brokenness in exchange for his life-altering love? Why don't we ask him to help us find a way to receive his love today?

Thursday

PRAYING IN LIGHT OF GOD'S LOVE

If I could speak all the languages of earth and of angels, but didn't love others, I would only be a noisy gong or a clanging cymbal. If I had the gift of prophecy, and if I understood all of God's secret plans and possessed all knowledge, and if I had such faith that I could move mountains, but didn't love others, I would be nothing. If I gave everything I have to the poor and even sacrificed my body, I could boast about it; but if I didn't love others, I would have gained nothing.

Love is patient and kind. Love is not jealous or boastful or proud or rude. It does not demand its own way. It is not irritable, and it keeps no record of being wronged. It does not rejoice about injustice but rejoices whenever the truth wins out. Love never gives up, never loses faith, is always hopeful, and endures through every circumstance. . . .

Three things will last forever—faith, hope, and love—and the greatest of these is love.   1 CORINTHIANS 13:1-7, 13

Reflect On: 1 Corinthians 13:1-7, 13
Praise God: For showing us what love is
Offer Thanks: That the greatest of all virtues is love
Confess: Any hostility that keeps you from proclaiming the gospel with love
Ask God: To increase your love for those who disagree with you

My aunt and uncle had a cabin in northern Michigan. It was a great place to visit, especially in warm weather when we could swim or fish in the river. One summer, when I was fourteen, my uncle purchased an old wreck to drive around in the woods. I was surprised when he handed me the keys, assuring me that I—who had never been behind the wheel of a car—couldn't possibly damage it. Treating it more like a tank than a car, I gladly took the wheel. Sadly, my excursion ended when the car refused to budge after running over a large stump. I'm not much of a mechanic, but I think it may have been the universal joint.

As you may know, a U-joint is a joint with hinges that enables the wheels to move. I think God's love is like that—it's what drives the Christian life. Without it, faith devolves into dead religion with no power to change anyone, except perhaps for the worse.

Writing in the *New York Times* about the decline of evangelicalism in the United States, John S. Dickerson says, "Some evangelical leaders are embarrassed by our movement's present paralysis. I am not. Weakness is a potent purifier. As Paul wrote, 'I am content with weaknesses . . . for the sake of Christ' (2 Corinthians 12:10). For me, the deterioration and disarray of the movement is a source of hope: hope that churches will stop angling for human power and start proclaiming the power of Christ." He notes that Christians "cannot change ancient doctrines to adapt to the currents of the day. But," he says, "we can, and must, adapt the way we hold our beliefs—with grace and humility instead of superior hostility. The core evangelical belief is that love and forgiveness are freely available to all who trust in Jesus Christ. This is the 'good news' from which the evangelical name originates ('euangelion' is a Greek word meaning 'glad tidings' or 'good news'). Instead of offering hope, many evangelicals have claimed the role of moral gatekeeper, judge and jury. If we continue in that posture, we will continue to invite opposition and obscure the 'good news' we are called to proclaim."[1]

Dickerson's analysis applies to Christians from every branch of the church. Without love, the Good News doesn't sound very good. Only God's love can effectively transmit the gospel to others. It's what enables people to experience his transforming grace.

Friday

PROMISES ASSOCIATED WITH GOD'S LOVE

I was standing in the aisle after boarding the airplane, wondering why the line had stopped snaking forward. Looking toward the middle of the plane, I spotted the problem. A middle-aged man was doing his best to stuff an oversize bag into the bin above his seat. He kept pushing, shoving, pressing, squashing, and punching the bag as though sheer determination would make it smaller than it was. Those of us waiting in line behind him were getting restless. It was hard to believe he couldn't admit the obvious: there was no way that particular bag would ever fit into that particular space. Finally, an airline attendant took pity on everyone by simply checking the bag.

That experience made me think of how foolish it is to keep trying failed strategies despite evidence that they never work. Take the strategy of trying to make yourself acceptable to God—of trying to clean yourself up or behave your way into his good graces. No matter how hard or how long you try, you will never succeed. God's love isn't a prize to be earned but a gift to be received. You have to admit that you don't deserve to be loved but that you need to be loved. Getting to that place requires honesty and humility.

Putting God off until you "get your act together" is like telling the doctor you will make an appointment as soon as you are well. You will never get well without God's help.

C. S. Lewis says that the Christian "does not think God will love us because we are good, but that God will make us good because He loves us."[2] Let's ask God today for the grace to receive everything he wants to give, believing that his love will make us who we want to be.

Promises in Scripture

> Some wandered in the wilderness,
> lost and homeless.
> Hungry and thirsty,
> they nearly died.
> "LORD, help!" they cried in their trouble,
> and he rescued them from their distress.
> He led them straight to safety,
> to a city where they could live.
> Let them praise the Lord for his great love
> and for the wonderful things he has done
> for them.
> For he satisfies the thirsty
> and fills the hungry with good things.
>
> Some sat in darkness and deepest gloom,
> imprisoned in iron chains of misery.
> They rebelled against the words of God,
> scorning the counsel of the Most High.
> That is why he broke them with hard labor;
> they fell, and no one was there to help them.
> "LORD, help!" they cried in their trouble,
> and he saved them from their distress.
> He led them from the darkness and deepest gloom;
> he snapped their chains.
> Let them praise the Lord for his great love
> and for the wonderful things he has done
> for them.
> For he broke down their prison gates of bronze;
> he cut apart their bars of iron.
>
> Some were fools; they rebelled
> and suffered for their sins.
> They couldn't stand the thought of food,

and they were knocking on death's door.
"LORD, help!" they cried in their trouble,
and he saved them from their distress.
He sent out his word and healed them,
snatching them from the door of death.
Let them praise the Lord for his great love
and for the wonderful things he has done
for them.

PSALM 107:4-21

The LORD your God is living among you.
He is a mighty savior.
He will take delight in you with gladness.
With his love, he will calm all your fears.
He will rejoice over you with joyful songs.

ZEPHANIAH 3:17

This is real love—not that we loved God, but that he loved us and
sent his Son as a sacrifice to take away our sins.

1 JOHN 4:10

Continued Prayer and Praise
Deuteronomy 6:4-6
Deuteronomy 7:6-11
Proverbs 3:12
Jeremiah 31:3
Hosea 11
Matthew 5:44-48
Matthew 22:36-40
Luke 7:44-48
John 16:27
John 17:22-26
Galatians 5:22

1 Timothy 6:10
1 John 2:15-17

2

GOD IS BETTER THAN YOU THINK

GOOD

His Nature

What word do you get when you subtract an *o* from the word *good*? *God*, of course. The Bible tells us that the God we worship contains no shadows but is thoroughly good (James 1:17). That means he is never arrogant, cowardly, greedy, lazy, vain, weak, irritable, moody, or envious. With no failings or flaws, he is far better than the best person you have ever met or read about. Because God is entirely good, there is never any room for improvement, never any need for change. Everything about him—his thoughts, motives, intentions, plans, words, commands, decisions, and actions—is good.

Key Scripture

Moses responded, "Then show me your glorious presence."

The Lord replied, "I will make all my goodness pass before you, and I will call out my name, Yahweh, before you. For I will show mercy to anyone I choose, and I will show compassion to anyone I choose."

EXODUS 33:18-19

Monday

GOD REVEALS HIMSELF

The LORD replied to Moses, "I will indeed do what you have asked, for I look favorably on you, and I know you by name."

Moses responded, "Then show me your glorious presence."

The LORD replied, "I will make all my goodness pass before you, and I will call out my name, Yahweh, before you. For I will show mercy to anyone I choose, and I will show compassion to anyone I choose. But you may not look directly at my face, for no one may see me and live." The LORD continued, "Look, stand near me on this rock. As my glorious presence passes by, I will hide you in the crevice of the rock and cover you with my hand until I have passed by. Then I will remove my hand and let you see me from behind. But my face will not be seen." . . .

Then the LORD came down in a cloud and stood there with him; and he called out his own name, Yahweh. The LORD passed in front of Moses, calling out,

> "Yahweh! The LORD!
> The God of compassion and mercy!
> I am slow to anger
>   and filled with unfailing love and faithfulness.
> I lavish unfailing love to a thousand generations.
>   I forgive iniquity, rebellion, and sin.
> But I do not excuse the guilty.
>   I lay the sins of the parents upon their children
>   and grandchildren;
> the entire family is affected—
>   even children in the third and fourth
>   generations."

EXODUS 33:17-23; 34:5-7

Understanding His Goodness

It's interesting to note that God's goodness, according to his self-disclosure to Moses, includes compassion, mercy, patience, unfailing love, and forgiveness—but also punishment. We warm to the initial list but freeze a little when we hear him say that not only does he not excuse the guilty, but he lays the sins of the parents on future generations. A similar warning is found in Exodus 20:5: "I lay the sins of the parents upon their children; the entire family is affected—even children in the third and fourth generations of those who reject me."

Perhaps it's not so surprising that God would allow people who continue to reject his goodness to suffer the consequences. Imagine, for instance, a man with children who pays no attention to God and in whom God's image is consequently marred. Over the course of his life, he may succumb to various temptations—becoming addicted to pornography, pride, drugs, sex, or alcohol. Or perhaps he's so attached to money that he becomes a workaholic. That father's behavior, whether it takes the form of abuse or neglect, is visited on his children. Because of his inability to reflect God's image, his children suffer consequences that may then be passed on to future generations.

Turning your back on God's goodness—on his kindness, his love, and his patience—is like choosing to move to the Arctic Circle when someone has just offered you a home in the Tropics. Of course, none of us can perfectly reflect God's goodness. But our commitment to Christ and to the work of his Spirit enables us to grow into his likeness.

In the Hebrew Scriptures the noun *tob* is translated as "good," "prosperity," or "good things" and is usually linked to material goods. The adjective version of this word pertains to beauty, goodness, and moral uprightness. In the New Testament, *agathos* is translated as "good," "kind," or "right," while the adjective *kalos* can be translated as "good," "better," "right," "what is good," or "beautiful."

Scripture makes clear that all goodness comes from God. Even though God's perfect world has been marred by sin, we see evidence of his goodness everywhere—in the beauty of nature, in the kindness of others, in the gifts he bestows. More specifically, Jesus came to preach the Good News to all who will listen. God's goodness is overflowing. As James says, "Whatever is good and perfect is a gift coming down to us from God our Father, who created all the lights in the heavens. He never changes or casts a shifting shadow" (1:17).

Lord, you have always been good to me. Thank you that out of the overflow of your goodness, I have experienced beauty, mercy, kindness, and grace. Let me begin each day with thankfulness for who you are and for all that you have done.

Studying His Goodness

1. Close your eyes and imagine you are Moses having a conversation with God. You feel a thrill at his promise, "I will make all my goodness pass before you." Stay in God's presence. What do you see?
2. God says he will "lavish unfailing love to a thousand generations," but he also warns that he will inflict consequences even to "children in the third and fourth generations" of the guilty. What do you make of this distinction?
3. Think of the person you know who best reflects God's goodness. List his or her qualities.
4. Make a list of all the ways God has revealed his goodness to you.
5. Have you ever been tempted to think that God isn't always good? What were the circumstances?

Tuesday

PRAYING IN LIGHT OF GOD'S GOODNESS

God created human beings in his own image.
In the image of God he created them;
male and female he created them.

Then God blessed them and said, "Be fruitful and multiply. Fill the
earth and govern it. Reign over the fish in the sea, the birds in the sky,
and all the animals that scurry along the ground." . . .
  Then God looked over all he had made, and he saw that it was
very good!

GENESIS 1:27-28, 31

Reflect On: Genesis 1:27-31
Praise God: Because from the overflow of his goodness, he created the world
Offer Thanks: That God has created you in his image, making you a person who is capable of loving and being loved
Confess: Your inability, without his grace, to consistently love God and others
Ask God: To send his love into the world through you

If God is good, why _____?

  Fill in the blank however you see fit. Our doubts about God's goodness are natural, given the kind of world we live in. If we grant that God is both all good and all powerful, why does he often fail to prevent evil?

Perhaps there is no answer that will satisfy people reeling from an incursion of evil into their lives or into the lives of those they love. Healing requires time. Even so, we must attempt at least a partial answer, lest we be forced to admit a falsehood—that there are limits to God's power, knowledge, and goodness.

Before we can begin to understand why God allows evil in the world, we need to talk about what would happen if he didn't. Perhaps you've seen a sci-fi movie whose plot revolves around an automaton—a "person or animal that acts in a monotonous, routine manner, without active intelligence." Such movies can be horrifying precisely because of what happens when humans lose their ability to think and choose. If God were to eradicate evil from our world, there would be no such thing as human beings but only highly sophisticated automatons programmed to do his will.

If you want to know why a good God would allow evil, let me offer a one-word answer. *Love.* God allows evil so that love can flourish. Though love doesn't cause evil, it makes evil possible. Why? Because God's original purpose in creating humans was to create beings with a capacity to love. But love can be neither coerced nor commanded. It has to be given freely, or it is not love but bondage.

Being free to love means that we are also free to reject love and to act in unloving, evil ways toward God and others. Remember what Jesus said: "If you love me, obey my commandments" (John 14:15). The failure to love God enough to obey him is what fractured the world in the very beginning, opening it to a host of evils. Though evil can present itself as a terrifying, all-destroying power, it starts out as merely a maladaptive response to God's invitation to love. Our refusal is what opens the door to evil of every kind.

Yes, God could have created us without the capacity to love.

And he could have made evil impossible. But then we would be robots, forced to do his will because we could not choose to do otherwise.

As you ponder God's goodness today, ask for the grace to respond lovingly to whatever he asks you to do.

Wednesday

PRAYING IN LIGHT OF GOD'S GOODNESS

[Joseph's brothers] sent this message to Joseph: "Before your father died, he instructed us to say to you: 'Please forgive your brothers for the great wrong they did to you—for their sin in treating you so cruelly.' So we, the servants of the God of your father, beg you to forgive our sin." When Joseph received the message, he broke down and wept. Then his brothers came and threw themselves down before Joseph. "Look, we are your slaves!" they said.

But Joseph replied, "Don't be afraid of me. Am I God, that I can punish you? You intended to harm me, but God intended it all for good. He brought me to this position so I could save the lives of many people."

GENESIS 50:16-20

Reflect On:	Genesis 50:14-24
Praise God:	For his power to turn his good intentions into reality
Offer Thanks:	Because God always intends your good
Confess:	Any accusations you have made that would call God's goodness into question
Ask God:	To help you trust more deeply in his goodness

"Okay, that's a dollar."

"What, just because I called somebody stupid, you're going to charge me a dollar? If you loved me, you wouldn't punish me. That's not fair!"

I've had this conversation, or one like it, more than once after

31

fining my children for calling people names. I think of the dollar as a symbolic pinch—a small discomfort to get their attention so they'll stop doing what they shouldn't. But sometimes protests erupt, and out comes the canard about punishment and love being incompatible.

The "if you loved me" argument can intrude into our own notions about God's goodness. *If you loved me, you wouldn't let me lose my job, go through a divorce, become ill. If you loved me, I'd have enough money to buy a house, go to college, retire.* The trouble with this "if you loved me" habit is that it can erode our sense of how good God has already been to us and how his goodness will ultimately triumph in our lives.

I wonder if Joseph, the one with the multicolored coat, ever asked the "if you loved me" question. If anyone had a right to ask, surely it was Joseph, who as a boy had been sold into slavery in Egypt, betrayed by brothers who were jealous of him. It's a wonderful story, but it wouldn't have felt wonderful to Joseph when he was violently separated from the father who loved him and later thrown into an Egyptian prison for a crime he didn't commit. Who would blame him for questioning God's goodness in such circumstances?

Though we don't know whether Joseph ever asked the question, we do know how he answered it many years later when his brothers begged his forgiveness. By then Joseph had become a ruler in Egypt—a man of great power. His answer came through tears: "You intended to harm me, but God intended it all for good."

No matter what harm comes to us—and harm will come—we need to ask God to help us understand that even though others may intend harm, God intends all of it—every drop of it—for our good and the good of others. His intentions matter, not simply because they are good, but because he has the power to turn those good intentions into reality.

The next time you find yourself in trouble, resist the temptation to wave an "if only you loved me" banner over your life. Instead, hold up a sign that reads, "God intends it all for good." Because he does.

Thursday

PRAYING IN LIGHT OF GOD'S GOODNESS

O people, the Lord has told you what is good,
and this is what he requires of you:
to do what is right, to love mercy,
and to walk humbly with your God.
Fear the Lord if you are wise!
His voice calls to everyone in Jerusalem:
"The armies of destruction are coming;
the Lord is sending them."

MICAH 6:8-9

Reflect On: Micah 6:8-9; Psalm 139
Praise God: For giving you the grace to know what is good
Offer Thanks: For all the good God has accomplished
through you
Confess: Any tendency to let your opinions of what is
right be influenced more by the culture than
by God's Word
Ask God: To give you courage to speak up for what is right

Recently I was watching a favorite program—a mystery set in a Scandinavian country. Though I loved the artistry of the program, something about it was profoundly unsettling. What bothered me was the way it portrayed a group of Christians at the heart of the mystery. Admittedly the group was weird and off base. Okay, there *are* groups of Christians who are weird and off base. No objection there.

But what initially made the group seem like fanatics to the

Swedish authorities was that its members opposed homosexuality and abortion, the inference being that these are extremist positions. However, for most of its two-thousand-year history, the church—whether Protestant, Catholic, or Orthodox— has always upheld biblical standards for marriage and life. The implied assumption of the program was that anyone who adheres to the historic Christian faith must be an extremist. How is it that a society formerly rooted in Judeo-Christian values could slip so far from them?

C. S. Lewis believed there is often one qualification for knowing what is good, and that is being good. Here's how he explained it: "When a man is getting better he understands more and more clearly the evil that is still left in him. When a man is getting worse, he understands his own badness less and less. . . . You understand sleep when you are awake, not while you are sleeping. . . . You can understand the nature of drunkenness when you are sober, not when you are drunk."[1] This observation can be applied to culture as well as to individuals. The more a culture leans toward what is bad, the less it recognizes what is good. Conversely, the more it advances toward goodness, the more maladies it recognizes within itself that still need to be fixed. This is true whether the problems are rooted in sexual immorality or rampant greed.

Today, when many are embracing the myth that progress lies along the lines of moral relativism, we need to pray for the grace both to *be* good and to *know* good. Join me in asking God to raise up powerful voices who are not afraid to speak into the culture, so that together we will know what is good—and then do it.

Friday

PROMISES ASSOCIATED WITH GOD'S GOODNESS

Have you ever listened to a speech as it was being translated? Some translators are so adept you hardly notice they are there. Good translators can make split-second decisions that accurately communicate the speaker's intent. Perhaps it's my suspicious nature, but I've sometimes wondered whether it might be possible for a translator in a sensitive political situation to purposely escalate tensions by inserting a mistranslated word here and there.

When it comes to God's promised goodness, I wonder if some of us have fallen for a sabotaged version of the truth. The psalmist says, "Surely your goodness and unfailing love will pursue me all the days of my life, and I will live in the house of the LORD forever" (Psalm 23:6). But our fear tells us that the only thing that will pursue us is trouble.

The prophet Nahum also speaks of God's goodness: "The LORD is good, a strong refuge when trouble comes. He is close to those who trust in him" (Nahum 1:7). And yet we struggle to trust him in the midst of the challenges we face.

Let's ask God to bless us today with the best translator in the world—the Holy Spirit, who can help us consider God's Word and apply it to our lives. Let's finish our prayer for God's blessing by singing words from John Newton's hymn "Amazing Grace":

The Lord has promised good to me,
His word my hope secures;
He will my shield and portion be
As long as life endures.

Promises in Scripture

> How great is the goodness
>   you have stored up for those who fear you.
> You lavish it on those who come to you for protection,
>   blessing them before the watching world.

PSALM 31:19

The Holy Spirit produces this kind of fruit in our lives: love, joy, peace, patience, kindness, goodness, faithfulness, gentleness, and self-control. There is no law against these things!

GALATIANS 5:22-23

Whatever is good and perfect is a gift coming down to us from God our Father, who created all the lights in the heavens. He never changes or casts a shifting shadow.

JAMES 1:17

Continued Prayer and Praise

Genesis 3:1-5
2 Chronicles 7:1-3
Psalm 106:1
Psalm 145:8-9
Matthew 5:45-48
Luke 18:18-30
Romans 8:28-30
Romans 12:2

3

GOD IS BIGGER
THAN YOU THINK

INFINITE

His Nature

Because of our own limitations, it's easy for us human beings to try to shrink God down to size, imagining he is far smaller than he is. We wonder, for instance, if he is big enough to deal with the world's intractable problems or even with our own most painful difficulties. But if we conceive of him as simply a larger, better version of ourselves, then we are not thinking of the God of the Bible.

Though none of us can fathom God's greatness, we can come to know him better by considering what Scripture reveals about his infinite nature, realizing that everything about him—his love, grace, mercy, and power—is immeasurably greater than anything we could ask or imagine.

Key Scripture

> Great is the LORD! He is most worthy of praise!
> No one can measure his greatness.
>
> PSALM 145:3

Monday

GOD REVEALS HIMSELF

Will God really live on earth? Why, even the highest heavens cannot contain you. How much less this Temple I have built!

1 KINGS 8:27

> Great is the LORD! He is most worthy of praise!
>   No one can measure his greatness.

PSALM 145:3

> Have you never heard?
>   Have you never understood?
> The LORD is the everlasting God,
>   the Creator of all the earth.
> He never grows weak or weary.
>   No one can measure the depths
>   of his understanding.

ISAIAH 40:28

Understanding His Infinity

By saying that God is infinite, we are saying it is impossible to measure him. He is without beginning or end and has no length, width, height, or depth. Neither space nor time can contain him. He is without boundaries or limitations. Since he is not made up of parts, he cannot be subtracted from or added to. He is completely himself, enjoying infinite wisdom, power, perfection, justice, love, mercy, and goodness. All his attributes are infinite. He is immense, incalculable, unfathomable. His wisdom is unsearchable.

Recognizing how difficult it is for finite creatures to think about an infinite God, A. W. Tozer puts it this way: "You may have a charley horse in your head for two weeks after trying to follow this, but it's a mighty good cure for this little cheap god we have today. This little cheap god we've made up is one you can pal around with—'the Man upstairs,' the fellow who helps you win baseball games. That god isn't the God of Abraham, Isaac and Jacob. He isn't the God who laid the foundations of the heaven and the earth; he's some other god."[1]

Listen to how *The Message* interprets Job 36:26: "Take a long, hard look. See how great he is—infinite, greater than anything you could ever imagine or figure out!" Though most Bible translations rarely use the word *infinite*, the idea of a God of infinite majesty and greatness is threaded throughout Scripture. The most extraordinary mind, the most powerful imagination cannot begin to picture how great our God is.

Great and holy God, there is no one like you. Today I bow before you, humbled to be called into your presence. Let me magnify you. Make my life an anthem of praise to you.

Studying His Infinity

1. Take a moment to look at your surroundings. Is there anything within your range of vision that could not be measured, provided you had the proper tools?
2. When Solomon dedicated the Temple in Jerusalem, his prayer recorded in 1 Kings seems almost incredulous, expressing a sense of wonder that God would choose to dwell in an earthly temple. How can an infinite God be present on earth?
3. Comment on ways people try to measure God. How might this tendency affect their faith?
4. Though creatures are, by definition, limited, the Creator is not. What are the implications of God's infinite nature in terms of his energy, power, understanding, and love?

Tuesday

PRAYING IN LIGHT OF GOD'S INFINITY

Will God really live on earth? Why, even the highest heavens cannot contain you. How much less this Temple I have built!

1 KINGS 8:27

We are the temple of the living God. As God said:

> *"I will live in them*
> *and walk among them.*
> *I will be their God,*
> *and they will be my people."*

2 CORINTHIANS 6:16

Reflect On: 1 Kings 8:27; 2 Corinthians 6:16
Praise God: For his infinite love
Offer Thanks: That God wants to dwell in you
Confess: Any sinful ways of trying to satisfy your desires
Ask God: To fill you with greater longing for him

Do you remember the opening lines of *Star Trek?* The latest version went like this:

Space . . . the Final Frontier. These are the voyages of the starship *Enterprise.* Her ongoing mission: to explore strange new worlds, to seek out new life forms and new civilizations, to boldly go where no one has gone before.

45

The quest to understand the concept of God's infinity involves undertaking a spiritual mission, the motto of which could be "to boldly go where few have gone before." The quest stretches us because it is impossible to fathom a being who operates without the constraints of time or space.

Unlike the crew of the starship *Enterprise*, we can rely on the help of guides who have undertaken this mission before us. One of these is Augustine, the fourth-century theologian and bishop who once famously expressed his longing for God by saying, "You have made us for yourself, and our hearts are restless until they find their rest in you."

"What place is there in me," he asked, "to which my God can come, what place that can receive the God who made heaven and earth? Does this mean, O Lord my God, that there is in me something fit to contain you?"

Centuries later, the seventeenth-century mathematician and philosopher Blaise Pascal took the question a step further, asking, "What else does this craving, and this helplessness proclaim but that there was once in man a true happiness, of which all that now remains is the empty print and trace?"[2] He goes on to speak of an "infinite abyss" that can be filled only with something that is itself infinite—with God himself.

To put it plainly, there exists in each of us an insatiable space—an infinite abyss—that we try without success to fill, stuffing it with pleasure, power, money, or sex. But nothing works. The hole remains.

It has been said, falsely, that Alexander the Great wept because there were no more worlds to conquer. The story endures despite its falsehood because it captures our sense that we have been created with insatiable desires.

What if the abyss Pascal speaks of—this "empty print and trace"—was left there by God, not because he wants us to remain forever unsatisfied, but because he intends to satisfy us with his presence? What if the happiness we seek can be found only when God is resident within us?

Today, as you pray, thank God for his infinite humility in deciding to dwell in the unlikeliest of places—within the confines of the human heart.

Wednesday

PRAYING IN LIGHT OF GOD'S INFINITY

> I will exalt you, my God and King,
>> and praise your name forever and ever.
> I will praise you every day;
>> yes, I will praise you forever.
> Great is the LORD! He is most worthy of praise!
>> No one can measure his greatness.
>
> PSALM 145:1-3

Reflect On: Psalm 145
Praise God: For his great majesty
Offer Thanks: That no one is as great as he is
Confess: Any tendency to treat God too casually
Ask God: To increase your awe in his presence

At the G20 summit in London, the president of the United States was criticized for bowing to Saudi Arabia's King Abdullah. By deferring to royalty in a gesture of subservience, critics said, his action broke with centuries of American tradition.

In *Miss Manners' Guide to Excruciatingly Correct Behavior, Freshly Updated,* Judith Martin, aka Miss Manners, states that American women who curtsy to royalty are "in error, not only in the matter of world etiquette, but of geography, physics, and ancient and modern history."[3] According to Miss Manners and others, Americans do not bow, curtsy, genuflect, or otherwise show obeisance in the presence of royalty. For us, a handshake is enough to show respect.

Americans are not famous for their deference to royalty. By

contrast, many Jewish people show reverence for God by refusing to pronounce his covenant name[4] except when praying or studying the Torah. Afraid to profane his name, various rabbinical writers have called it "the great and terrible Name," "the unutterable Name," "the ineffable Name," "the distinguished Name," "the holy Name," or simply "the Name." Rather than saying God's name in Hebrew, they substitute *Adonai*, meaning "Lord," or *Ha-shem*, meaning "the Name." Even in English, they write the name as "G-d." They do this out of fear that God's name could be defaced or destroyed if it were to appear in written form.

You probably know that the mathematical sign for infinity looks like this:

But when it comes to God, I like to think that the dash between the letters of his English name "G-d" symbolizes infinity, speaking to us of the mystery that resides within his nature. G-d's ways, Scripture tells us, are unsearchable. As the heavens are higher than the earth, his thoughts are higher than our thoughts.

So, with the knowledge that God is infinite, how should we enter his presence? We should do the only thing that makes sense—bow down and worship the one whose greatness can never be measured.

Thursday

PRAYING IN LIGHT OF GOD'S INFINITY

Joyful are those who have the God of Israel
*   as their helper,*
* whose hope is in the LORD their God.*
He made heaven and earth,
*   the sea, and everything in them.*
*   He keeps every promise forever.*
He gives justice to the oppressed
*   and food to the hungry.*
The LORD frees the prisoners.
*   The LORD opens the eyes of the blind.*
The LORD lifts up those who are
*   weighed down.*
*   The LORD loves the godly.*
The LORD protects the foreigners among us.
*   He cares for the orphans and widows,*
*   but he frustrates the plans of the wicked.*

The LORD will reign forever.
*   He will be your God, O Jerusalem,*
*   throughout the generations.*

PSALM 146:5-10

Reflect On:	Psalm 146:5-10
Praise God:	Because he keeps every promise forever
Offer Thanks:	That God is your helper
Confess:	Any doubts you have about God's ability or willingness to care for you
Ask God:	To help you understand his heart for those in need

Everyone named Sandy must have felt insulted when their name was associated with one of the most brutal storms ever to hit the Northeast. In October 2012, Hurricane Sandy sent water surging over break walls, flooding subway tunnels, and wreaking havoc wherever water rushed in, killing more than forty people in New York City alone. Superstorms like Sandy remind us of the terrible power of the raging sea.

Sometimes our own lives are threatened by monster storms— overwhelming problems that threaten to drag us down. If we are not in the midst of a storm, we know of others who are. Your list of people might be as long as mine. Here's a small sample from my own life: I'm praying for a man who has been crushed by a business failure, someone battling brain cancer, a couple in the midst of a bitter divorce, a mother who suffers from dementia, a child with a mental illness. When life is intractably hard, it helps to recall the immensity of God, to remember that it is when we are weakest that God can show himself strongest.

"The temptations in your life," Paul told the Corinthians, "are no different from what others experience. And God is faithful. He will not allow the temptation to be more than you can stand. When you are tempted, he will show you a way out so that you can endure" (1 Corinthians 10:13). For many of us, our worst temptation is to doubt God. We find it difficult to trust in his love and count on his mercy. But trust we must, reminding ourselves that nothing is impossible for a God of infinite greatness.

Your problems, however large they loom, are not too big for God to handle. Even if the things you fear most come to pass, God will be with you, holding you up and keeping you safe, so that with Paul you will say, "I am convinced that nothing can ever separate me from God's love. Neither death nor life, neither angels nor demons, neither my fears for today nor my worries about tomorrow—not even the powers of hell can separate me from God's love. No power in the sky above or in the earth below—indeed, nothing in all creation will ever be able to separate me from the love of God that is revealed in Christ Jesus our Lord."[5] Amen.

Friday

PROMISES ASSOCIATED WITH GOD'S INFINITY

Imagine you are fighting for your life, facing an enemy whose one aim is to annihilate you. As you look across enemy lines, you are terrified by the forces lined up against you. But then you shift your focus to your side of the battle line. In front of you stands God, surrounded by the armies of heaven. You realize that the fight is not primarily about you but about whose kingdom is going to prevail. Looking at God, you know that no matter how fiercely the battle rages, his side will win because he is infinitely greater than the opposing forces.

Jesus' beloved friend John assured the early Christians that they would prevail, not through their own strength, but because the Spirit who lived within them was greater than the spirit who lived in the world (1 John 4:4).

The same is true for us. John's words urge us to focus on victory, not defeat. How do we do this? One way is to heed the psalmist's call to magnify the Lord and exalt his name (Psalm 34:3, ESV). When you magnify something, you make it look bigger. Since it's impossible to make God any bigger than he is, magnifying him means focusing on him in a way that enables you and others to perceive his immensity and greatness.

Failing to magnify God means that we will inevitably magnify our problems and complaints, making them seem bigger than they are. The former is a strategy for victory, and the latter for defeat. Today, let's celebrate the fact that we belong to the God who has numbered the stars in the sky and calls them all by name. We have the victory not because our foes are weak but because our God is infinitely strong.

Promises in Scripture

He counts the stars
   and calls them all by name.
How great is our Lord! His power is absolute!
   His understanding is beyond comprehension!

PSALM 147:4-5

"To whom will you compare me?
   Who is my equal?" asks the Holy One.

Look up into the heavens.
   Who created all the stars?
He brings them out like an army, one after another,
   calling each by its name.
Because of his great power and incomparable
     strength,
   not a single one is missing.
O Jacob, how can you say the LORD does not see
     your troubles?
   O Israel, how can you say God ignores your rights?
Have you never heard?
   Have you never understood?
The LORD is the everlasting God,
   the Creator of all the earth.
He never grows weak or weary.
   No one can measure the depths of his
     understanding.
He gives power to the weak
   and strength to the powerless.
Even youths will become weak and tired,
   and young men will fall in exhaustion.
But those who trust in the LORD will find new
     strength.

> They will soar high on wings like eagles.
> They will run and not grow weary.
> They will walk and not faint.

ISAIAH 40:25-31

You belong to God, my dear children. You have already won a victory over those people, because the Spirit who lives in you is greater than the spirit who lives in the world.

1 JOHN 4:4

Continued Prayer and Praise

Exodus 15:1-18
Job 40
Psalm 113
Psalm 145:4-21
Ephesians 3:20-21

4

GOD IS
NOT MOODY

UNCHANGEABLE, IMMUTABLE

His Nature

We live in a world that is always changing, among people whose moods can be mercurial. That makes it difficult for us to conceive of a being who will never change. But Scripture tells us it is impossible for God to change. He can't grow stronger or weaker, nor can he grow better or worse. Neither can he waver between two opinions. That's because God is already everything he should be; his nature and his will are unchanging, immutable. But that doesn't make him rigid, unbending, temperamental, or unpredictable—far from it. The unchangeable nature of his character assures us that he can always be relied on. He is the rock upon which we stand.

Key Scripture

Whatever is good and perfect is a gift coming down to us from God our Father, who created all the lights in the heavens. He never changes or casts a shifting shadow.

JAMES 1:17

Monday

GOD REVEALS HIMSELF

I am the LORD, and I do not change.

MALACHI 3:6

Jesus Christ is the same yesterday, today, and forever. So do not be attracted by strange, new ideas.

HEBREWS 13:8-9

Whatever is good and perfect is a gift coming down to us from God our Father, who created all the lights in the heavens. He never changes or casts a shifting shadow.

JAMES 1:17

Understanding His Unchangeable Character

To say that God never changes is not to say that he doesn't shift his strategies to account for changing realities here on earth. Nothing precludes him from altering the way he accomplishes his purposes. And it's not to say that he does not allow himself to be moved by our prayers.

God's immutability applies to his character and to his will. He always hates sin but longs for sinners to return to him. He is always just, but his justice is tempered by mercy. He is always powerful, whether or not he displays that power. He is always loving, omniscient, near, forgiving, and wise. His attributes never change.

Though God is not predictable, it's possible to predict certain things about his character because of what he has already told us about himself. As his followers, we need to hold on to the truth so that when circumstances paint him as unloving, weak, or uncaring, our response will not be to revise our opinion of God;

rather, it will be to doubt the evidence, realizing its insufficiency to prove him other than who he is.

Though it's good to realize that God never changes because he's already perfect, we need to recognize that immutability would be a disaster for human beings. If we were immutable, we would be frozen in our imperfections. Instead, we can become more like the Christ we love. As difficult as change can be, it is an opportunity we can embrace. For the believer, two things make change possible: obedience to Christ and the power of the Holy Spirit at work within us.

If we refuse to change in the ways God asks, we will inevitably change for the worse. At such times some people begin to demand that God be the one to change. Offended by commandments that contradict certain cultural values, they insist God's standards are no longer valid. But to try to get God to change so we can remain the same is foolish. It's like running your car full speed into the side of a mountain, hoping the mountain will move.

Instead of demanding that God change, we should admit that we are the ones who need to be different. We should pray that his transforming grace will reshape our minds and hearts until everything about us reflects more of his unchanging goodness.

Lord, you are the immutable God who set the changing universe in motion. I praise you for always being exactly who you say you are. I can rest in this knowledge, secure in the fact that you never change or cast a shifting shadow.

Studying His Unchangeable Character

1. Though God's nature and will are unchanging, our understanding of him can change. Describe ways in which your picture of God has changed over the years.

2. How has your relationship with the unchanging God changed you?
3. The writer of Hebrews reminds his readers that Jesus is the same yesterday, today, and forever and then warns them against "strange, new ideas." What are some strange ideas you have encountered that do not align with God's Word? How did you respond?
4. James tells believers that "whatever is good and perfect" comes to us from God. Have you ever been tempted to blame God for things that are bad and imperfect? What were the circumstances?
5. How does knowing that God's will and nature never change affect your view of current circumstances? What are the implications for the way you will respond to your circumstances in the future?

Tuesday

PRAYING IN LIGHT OF GOD'S UNCHANGEABLE CHARACTER

God has said,

> *"I will never fail you.*
> *I will never abandon you."*

So we can say with confidence,

> *"The LORD is my helper,*
> *so I will have no fear.*
> *What can mere people do to me?"*

HEBREWS 13:5-6

Reflect On: Hebrews 13:5-6
Praise God: For his absolute integrity
Offer Thanks: Because God is your helper
Confess: Any tendency to judge God by human understanding
Ask God: To increase your sense of confidence and trust

I was standing in line at the counter, behind a customer who seemed to be taking his sweet time. My back had been aching for days, making it difficult to stand. I could feel the pain spreading, working its way up to my head and into my mouth. Yes, my mouth! It was everything I could do to keep from lambasting the man and the clerk assisting him. Later, after the pain had subsided, I realized how distorted my perspective had been. I had been kept waiting for only a couple of minutes—nothing to complain about. But the discomfort I felt had blackened my mood and muddled my thinking.

My ill temper was like an itchy trigger finger, waiting to blast whoever crossed my path.

Because we are subject to moods, it's no wonder we sometimes project our own fickleness onto God. We wonder if he's capricious—impulsive, unpredictable, and irritable—as we sometimes are. Do we have to walk on eggshells, lest we inadvertently offend him?

Thirteenth-century theologian Thomas Aquinas said that God has no potential to be anything other than who he is. That means his nature is fixed. His attributes do not change. Because he is perfect, God is already everything he should be. He can't devolve, even for a moment, which means it's impossible for him to lose perspective or control. It's also impossible for him to act in ways that contradict his purposes, plans, or promises.

The prophet Jonah knew this. That's why he ran when God commanded him to announce judgment on a city he despised. Instead of jumping at the chance to proclaim the bad news to Nineveh, Jonah tried to escape from God. It wasn't that his heart was suddenly filled with compassion for the Ninevites. Jonah ran because he didn't want to deliver a message that might inspire his enemies to repent. He knew that if that happened, God would be true to his nature, extending mercy to them.

Here's how Jonah explains himself: "Didn't I say before I left home that you would do this, LORD? That is why I ran away to Tarshish! I knew that you are a merciful and compassionate God, slow to get angry and filled with unfailing love. You are eager to turn back from destroying people. Just kill me now, LORD! I'd rather be dead" (Jonah 4:2-3).

Jonah is vindictive and histrionic, alternately terrified, happy, angry, and depressed, depending on the circumstances. But God

65

is the same throughout the story—a God of justice and mercy whose singular plan cannot be thwarted. This is the God we follow, the Lord we acclaim.

Today as you pray, thank God for always being exactly who he says he is—the same Lord yesterday, today, and forever.

Wednesday

PRAYING IN LIGHT OF GOD'S UNCHANGEABLE CHARACTER

We can be sure that we know him if we obey his commandments. If someone claims, "I know God," but doesn't obey God's commandments, that person is a liar and is not living in the truth. But those who obey God's word truly show how completely they love him. That is how we know we are living in him. Those who say they live in God should live their lives as Jesus did. . . . This world is fading away, along with everything that people crave. But anyone who does what pleases God will live forever.

1 JOHN 2:3-6, 17

Reflect On: 1 John 2:3-6, 17
Praise God: For his righteousness
Offer Thanks: Because God has shown you the way to live
Confess: Any tendency to condone what is against God's commands
Ask God: To help you express your love through obedience

Imagine that your feet are straddling a crack that is increasing at the rate of an eighth of an inch a month. By month six, it's still only a small gap, less than an inch. But after sixteen years, you're looking at two feet, and after forty years, the gap will have widened to five feet. It won't be long before you'll either fall into the gap or be forced to decide which side to stand on. To make things even more perilous, the gap is increasing at such a small annual rate, you hardly notice it.

That's a crude analogy, but it gives us a picture of our position as Christians living in societies in which Judeo-Christian values are steadily eroding.

For most people, change is difficult—agonizing even. One exception to that general rule might be the cultural decline that can occur stealthily and slowly, so slowly, in fact, that we barely notice it.

Many of the early Christians had an advantage we don't. They could clearly identify the radical distinction between Christianity and culture. Most of them lived in a world in which pagan gods were openly worshiped and in which brutality was the order of the day. The choice before them was obvious: Would they embrace the radical way of Christ or the way of a sin-darkened world?

Because many aspects of our culture still reflect Judeo-Christian values, our choices are not always as obvious. Some things about the culture are worth celebrating, but others are not. Living in a culture where tolerance is the most exalted virtue, we find it increasingly difficult to uphold clear standards of right and wrong. Afraid to disagree lest we be accused of self-righteousness, we remain silent. Some of us have gone further, discarding our values in favor of the feel-good values of our culture.

Increasingly, Christians seem little different from those around them. Whether it's cohabitation, divorce, materialism, or adopting a homosexual lifestyle, we Christians often look similar to our non-Christian neighbors.

Let me suggest a simple rule of thumb about how to respond to the growing gap between culture and Christianity: whenever there's a conflict between what the historic Christian faith has always taught and our own personal opinions, we should suspect the shaping influence of culture. In situations like these, we need to dig into Scripture and the teachings of Christianity as it's been practiced for more than two thousand years to determine what is right, not just what feels right. In the end, it's not

God who should submit to us but we who should submit to him. Because his standards don't change, neither should ours, no matter how much pressure we feel.

Pray for the grace to stand up today for what is right, but do it as Jesus would—hating the sin but loving the people who've committed it.

Thursday

PRAYING IN LIGHT OF GOD'S UNCHANGEABLE CHARACTER

The LORD your God is gracious and merciful. If you return to him, he will not continue to turn his face from you.

2 CHRONICLES 30:9

The faithful love of the LORD never ends!
     His mercies never cease.
Great is his faithfulness;
     his mercies begin afresh each morning.
I say to myself, "The LORD is my inheritance;
     therefore, I will hope in him!"

LAMENTATIONS 3:22-24

Reflect On: 2 Chronicles 30:9; Lamentations 3:22-24
Praise God: For his mercies, which are new every morning
Offer Thanks: For giving us the ability to change
Confess: Any unwillingness to change when you need to
Ask God: To help you repent

When one of my daughters was young, one of her favorite possessions was a lavishly illustrated book designed to teach young children about human anatomy. She would gaze with wonder at its overlapping transparent pages illustrating the skeletal system, then the muscles, and finally the circulatory system. Another favorite was a page containing an artist's rendition of a person progressing from fertilized egg to infancy, childhood, puberty, maturity, and old age.

That illustration reminds me of an obvious truth—that it's in the nature of created things to change. Without change, we would never realize our potential. Positive change, whether physical or moral, is a gift. While some of our transformations are delightful, like learning to utter our first words, others are dreadful, like slipping into dementia. Our souls change too—becoming more or less like Christ depending on our responses to him.

But God is not like us. As uncreated Spirit, he is not subject to change. He can never get better or worse. He is already everything he ought to be, everything he can be.

The Bible speaks clearly about our own need for radical change. Jesus came into our unstable, fallen world with the sole purpose of transforming our relationship with God and others. In this sense, change is our only hope. One of the main words the New Testament uses to help us understand the kind of change we need to embrace is the Greek word *metanoia*, or "repentance." The big idea behind metanoia is that of turning. We make a 180-degree turn away from sin so we can make a 180-degree turn toward God.

Though repentance can seem like a hard thing to do—something we dread—the result of true repentance is neither shame nor depression but a sense of lightness, relief, and joy. The sins that once burdened us are lifted by the grace of God. Repentance frees us so we can bask in his mercy rather than wallow in our sin. Though it's good to experience godly sorrow, the ultimate result of repentance is peace. The Shaker hymn "Simple Gifts" always makes me think of what true repentance feels like:

> 'Tis the gift to be simple, 'tis the gift to be free
> 'Tis the gift to come down where we ought to be,
> And when we find ourselves in the place just right,

'Twill be in the valley of love and delight.
When true simplicity is gain'd,
To bow and to bend we shan't be asham'd,
To turn, turn will be our delight,
Till by turning, turning we come 'round right.[1]

What kind of change do you most need to embrace? Instead of resisting because you fear you can't change or because you don't want to, turn to God in trust, confessing your sins as often as you need to and then asking him to show you how to change.

Friday

PROMISES ASSOCIATED WITH GOD'S UNCHANGEABLE CHARACTER

Last week, a national for-profit college announced it would be closing its campus in a suburb near me. The announcement came as a complete surprise to students who wondered whether they would be able to complete their degree programs without moving to another campus. The implicit promise between college and student—that all who successfully completed their programs would be awarded degrees—was abruptly threatened.

Anyone who has ever gotten married, signed a mortgage, purchased insurance, or bought something with a warranty realizes that a promise is only as reliable as the people or companies that make it.

Fortunately, the most important promises in our lives are ones God has made to us. He promises to forgive our sins, to never fail us or forsake us, to lift us up when we are bowed down, to lead us in the way of truth and life. But many of God's promises are conditional. Their fulfillment depends not on God's desire to keep his promises, but on our responses to them.

God will return to us *if* we return to him (Zechariah 1:3). We will find new strength *as* we trust in him (Ephesians 3:17). We will live in peace *if* we listen to God (Proverbs 1:33). God's desires for us, communicated through his promises, will never change. The question is, How will we respond to him?

Promises in Scripture

> *God is not a man, so he does not lie.*
> *He is not human, so he does not change*
> *his mind.*

> Has he ever spoken and failed to act?
> Has he ever promised and not carried it through?

NUMBERS 23:19

> All who listen to me will live in peace,
> untroubled by fear of harm.

PROVERBS 1:33

By his divine power, God has given us everything we need for living a godly life. We have received all of this by coming to know him, the one who called us to himself by means of his marvelous glory and excellence. And because of his glory and excellence, he has given us great and precious promises. These are the promises that enable you to share his divine nature and escape the world's corruption caused by human desires.

In view of all this, make every effort to respond to God's promises. Supplement your faith with a generous provision of moral excellence, and moral excellence with knowledge, and knowledge with self-control, and self-control with patient endurance, and patient endurance with godliness, and godliness with brotherly affection, and brotherly affection with love for everyone.

2 PETER 1:3-7

Continued Prayer and Praise
1 Samuel 15:29
Psalm 18:31
Psalm 102:12, 25-28
Isaiah 46:10
Hebrews 6:15-20
Hebrews 12:28

5

GOD IS
NOT WEAK

ALL POWERFUL, OMNIPOTENT

His Nature

"Power tends to corrupt, and absolute power corrupts absolutely."
The only being in the universe to whom Lord Acton's famous
proverb does not apply is God, in whom all power originates.
This means that God can do anything he wants, anytime he
wants, any way he wants. No force in the universe is strong
enough to stand against his power. All other power in our world
is derived from God, who shares his power. God is the only being
who is wise, strong, and loving enough to wield absolute power
in a way that is absolutely good.

Key Scripture

> *Powerful is your arm!*
> *Strong is your hand!*
> *Your right hand is lifted high in glorious strength.*
>
> PSALM 89:13

Monday

GOD REVEALS HIMSELF

Who in all of heaven can compare with the LORD?
    What mightiest angel is anything like the LORD?
The highest angelic powers stand in awe of God.
    He is far more awesome than all who surround
        his throne.
O LORD God of Heaven's Armies!
    Where is there anyone as mighty as you,
        O LORD?
    You are entirely faithful.

You rule the oceans.
    You subdue their storm-tossed waves. . . .

Powerful is your arm!
    Strong is your hand!
    Your right hand is lifted high in glorious
        strength. . . .

Happy are those who hear the joyful call
        to worship,
    for they will walk in the light of your
        presence, LORD.
They rejoice all day long in your wonderful
        reputation.
    They exult in your righteousness.
You are their glorious strength.
    It pleases you to make us strong.
Yes, our protection comes from the LORD,
    and he, the Holy One of Israel, has given
        us our king.

PSALM 89:6-9, 13, 15-18

79

Understanding His Power

What do a volcano and a fruit fly have in common? One thing, at least—the volcano's power to erupt and the bug's power to overcome gravity through flight both come from the hand of an all-powerful God. The Bible speaks of a God who is omnipotent—able to do anything. All other power in the universe is limited and derivative, coming as it does from God. From the first page of Scripture, which highlights God's creative power, to the last, which celebrates his triumphant power, we see a being to whom the words *unable*, *incompetent*, and *weak* never once apply.

Two biblical titles for God are closely associated with God's power: *El Shadday* (Genesis 17:1-2), usually translated "God Almighty," and *Yahweh-Tsebaoth* (1 Samuel 17:45), variously translated "the LORD Almighty," "the LORD of Heaven's Armies," or "the LORD of Hosts." In the New Testament, Paul calls Jesus the power of God (1 Corinthians 1:24). Toward the end of Matthew's Gospel, Jesus foretells a time in which he will return with "power and great glory" (24:30). And the book of Acts introduces us to the powerful work of God's Holy Spirit among believers (1:8).

Some have questioned the doctrine of God's omnipotence by saying that God cannot be all powerful since he can't do things contrary to logic or to his nature. For instance, he can't draw a circle in the shape of a square, and he can't sin, because that would contradict his goodness. To the more practical minded among us, such arguments seem a bit absurd. As C. S. Lewis has remarked, "It is no more possible for God than for the weakest of His creatures to carry out both of two mutually exclusive alternatives; not because His power meets an obstacle, but because nonsense remains nonsense even when we talk it about God."[1]

The New Testament word commonly translated as "power" is *dynamis*, from which the English words *dynamic* and *dynamite* come. This term describes the miracles, or acts of power, performed by Jesus, and it is also used to describe "the power of God that brings salvation" (Romans 1:16, NIV). The New Testament tells us that Christ's power is still available through his Holy Spirit, who shares it with us according to God's plan and purpose.

Another Greek word for power is *exousia*, which is often translated as "authority, power, right." Jesus had the authority, or the power, to forgive sins (Matthew 9:6-8). In Matthew's Gospel, Jesus tells his disciples that all authority in heaven and on earth has been given to him (28:18).

We can be glad that no other power can rival the power of God. He alone is omnipotent.

Lord, unlimited power is a difficult phrase to comprehend. Help me to grasp just how strong you are so I can glorify you by trusting in your power to save and uphold. Strengthen me today, I pray.

Studying His Power

1. Psalm 89 says it pleases God "to make us strong." Have you ever experienced a time in which God made you strong? If so describe it.
2. The psalmist implies that he rejoices all day long in God's "wonderful reputation" and that God is his "glorious strength." What might your life look like if you were able to do this every day?
3. Why is it sometimes difficult to believe that God is all powerful? What can you do to strengthen your faith during such times?

Tuesday

PRAYING IN LIGHT OF GOD'S POWER

It is not by force nor by strength, but by my Spirit, says the LORD of Heaven's Armies.

ZECHARIAH 4:6

We keep on praying for you, asking our God to enable you to live a life worthy of his call. May he give you the power to accomplish all the good things your faith prompts you to do. Then the name of our Lord Jesus will be honored because of the way you live, and you will be honored along with him. This is all made possible because of the grace of our God and Lord, Jesus Christ.

2 THESSALONIANS 1:11-12

Reflect On: Zechariah 4:6; 2 Thessalonians 1:11-12
Praise God: For the power of his Holy Spirit
Offer Thanks: That God shares his power through the Spirit
Confess: Any tendency to judge the motives of those who disagree with you
Ask God: To give you power to govern your tongue

As I write this, the political atmosphere is heating up once again. Great fissures have opened between the two parties vying for power in our country. Passions are white hot, with both sides looking for opportunities to trounce the opposition. The slightest misstep is eagerly pounced on and endlessly discussed. No one seems intent on searching for truth, because the game is not about truth but only about winning. Watching the news seems like an exercise in frustration because the media is all about spin.

Unfortunately, many Christians have allowed fissures to develop in their relationships with other believers because they do not see eye to eye on politics. Tragically, politics has sometimes trumped love within the Christian community. And it has hampered our witness to the world.

Though political policies can be of critical importance to the health of a nation, ultimately politics is pretty much an outside-in game—a power play by people who are certain their policies will transform the nation. And though Christians should be involved in all aspects of the political process, we must resist the political illusions that characterize our age.

The first illusion is that there is a political solution to every single problem we face. The second is that the most transformative power in the world is political in nature.

As Christians, we must realize that political power is both seductive and illusory. It promises more than it can deliver. Though it can do some things, it can't do all things. Quite often it cannot even begin to resolve our most difficult problems.

Unlike political power, the most profound power in the universe is one that operates not from the outside but from within. It's a power that can shape destinies and influence history. The power I am talking about is spiritual. It comes from God, not from society—and certainly not from any political party.

Think about the way you exercise power in your own life, particularly over yourself. How effective have you been in improving yourself simply by exerting your willpower? You may have experienced some limited success, breaking a bad habit or two, but without the transformative power of the Holy Spirit, you will never become the person you want to be and you will never do the things God is calling you to do. If we can't even change ourselves, who do we think we *can* change?

Today let's ask God to fill us with his Holy Spirit—the Spirit of wisdom and understanding, of counsel and might—so that we and those around us will become the kind of people who can build a society in which justice, truth, mercy, and goodness prevail. Let us not abdicate our political responsibilities; let us exercise them, serving in the power God gives.

Wednesday

PRAYING IN LIGHT OF GOD'S POWER

> O God, listen to my cry!
> Hear my prayer!
> From the ends of the earth,
> I cry to you for help
> when my heart is overwhelmed.
> Lead me to the towering rock of safety,
> for you are my safe refuge,
> a fortress where my enemies cannot
> reach me.
> Let me live forever in your sanctuary,
> safe beneath the shelter of your wings!
>
> PSALM 61:1-4

Reflect On: Psalm 61

Praise God: For his unbreakable strength

Offer Thanks: For God's absolute power over evil

Confess: Your tendency to rely on your own strength rather than his

Ask God: To help you experience him as your strong tower, your rock of safety

Have you ever wondered how L. Frank Baum came up with the name Oz? As in "the wonderful wizard of Oz"? According to Baum, one day he happened to glance at some file cabinets in his office, one of which was labeled O–Z. He discarded the dash, and the name Oz was born. But when Baum's widow was asked the same question, she insisted that her husband had simply plucked the name out of thin air, much as he'd done with the story of Dorothy and her visit to the Emerald City.

Neither answer has stopped speculation. Some say Baum chose Oz for its similarity to "Boz," the pseudonym of Charles Dickens; or he chose the "land of Oz" for its similarity to the "land of Uz," where the biblical Job lived; or he named Oz after "Ozymandias," a famous poem by Percy Bysshe Shelley.

Let me toss one more theory into the pot. Ōz is a Hebrew word meaning "strength, might, power." Perhaps Baum knew this and thought it the perfect name for a sham wizard who needed to project an outsize image for himself. Of course, this is pure speculation—nothing more. But in the Hebrew Scriptures, the word oz is often used to describe God's power or strength. One of God's titles is Migdal-Oz, which can be translated "strong tower." Psalm 61 says, "You have been my refuge, a strong tower against the foe" (v. 3, NIV).

Indeed God's power is always a refuge for believers. But if that is so, why do we sometimes feel our vulnerability so acutely, as though we're not residing in an impregnable tower, but standing in an open field with thousands of arrows pointed straight at us? Perhaps it's difficult to experience God's protection because we've unwittingly stepped outside the tower. We do that when we invest our trust elsewhere—in human relationships, in our own understanding, in our talents, or in our ability to provide for ourselves. But when the fragility of the things we rely on is revealed, what then?

In truth, God is the only one powerful enough to keep us safe. Let's not wait for our lives to collapse in order to learn how to trust him. Instead, let's ask today for the grace we need to begin sheltering in his strength.

Thursday

PRAYING IN LIGHT OF GOD'S POWER

Because of their unbelief, he couldn't do any miracles among them except to place his hands on a few sick people and heal them. And he was amazed at their unbelief.

MARK 6:5-6

Reflect On: Mark 6:1-6
Praise God: For the power of his Word
Offer Thanks: For all the ways God has displayed his power in your life
Confess: Any areas of unbelief
Ask God: To release his power in the church and in you

Throughout the course of his public ministry, Jesus performed incredible works of power. Here was a man who could do anything—turn water into wine, heal the deaf, cast out demons, raise the dead. Yet Scripture seems to indicate that his power could be impeded by an attitude of the heart the Bible calls "unbelief." Listen to this sobering comment from Mark's Gospel: "Because of their unbelief, he couldn't do any miracles among them."

Later in the same Gospel, Jesus rebukes a group of Sadducees for mocking belief in a physical resurrection. Striking directly at their unbelief, he says, "Your mistake is that you don't know the Scriptures, and you don't know the power of God" (12:24).

I wonder how many of us make the same mistake. The other day a friend implied that some unemployed Christians are so poor that they're forced to sell illicit drugs. It's the only way they can survive in a down economy. I don't want to be naive to the terrible challenges of poverty, but what about trusting in God's help? I know of pastors who are convinced that homosexuals can't change their behaviors or that unmarried heterosexuals can't live without sex. But what about God's grace to help us live the way Christ has shown us?

And what about our own lives? Are we selling God's power short, expecting too little of him? Have we given up on people who seem far from God, failing to pray with faith, believing God's light is stronger than the darkness that blinds them? Let's not allow sociology or political correctness or difficult circumstances or scientific progress to suffocate our faith in God and in his Word.

I don't know about you, but I long for more of God's power to be displayed in his church and in me. Let's ask God to help us recognize unbelief for what it is and stop indulging it. Let's commit ourselves to knowing Scripture and the power of God— not simply for our own sakes, but for the glory of our great and mighty God.

Friday

PROMISES ASSOCIATED WITH GOD'S POWER

I don't know about you, but I could do with a little more *stērizō*. What, you may wonder, is that? It's not an exotic drink nor a performance-enhancing supplement for athletes, but a Greek word used in the New Testament, meaning "to strengthen, fix something in place, establish, make strong." Sterizo is about being made strong on the inside so that no matter what we face, we can stand firm in hope and faith. What's more, we are to sterizo others, strengthening them as we have been strengthened.

When it came to sterizo, Paul was a champion. But he shared his strength in a surprising way: by boasting of his weakness. Why? Because he was certain that his weakness was the conduit for God's strength (2 Corinthians 12:1-10).

If you feel weak today, don't wallow in your weakness but thank God for it, asking him to use it as a pathway for sterizo.

Promises in Scripture

> The LORD is my strength and shield.
>> I trust him with all my heart.
> He helps me, and my heart is filled
>> with joy.
>> I burst out in songs of thanksgiving.

> The LORD gives his people strength.
>> He is a safe fortress for his anointed
>> king.

PSALM 28:7-8

All glory to God, who is able to make you strong.

ROMANS 16:25

To keep me from becoming proud, I was given a thorn in my flesh, a messenger from Satan to torment me and keep me from becoming proud.

Three different times I begged the Lord to take it away. Each time he said, "My grace is all you need. My power works best in weakness." So now I am glad to boast about my weaknesses, so that the power of Christ can work through me. That's why I take pleasure in my weaknesses, and in the insults, hardships, persecutions, and troubles that I suffer for Christ. For when I am weak, then I am strong.

2 CORINTHIANS 12:7-10

May he . . . make your hearts strong, blameless, and holy as you stand before God our Father when our Lord Jesus comes again with all his holy people.

1 THESSALONIANS 3:13

Continued Prayer and Praise
Deuteronomy 4:32-39
Psalm 49:14-15
Matthew 28:18
Acts 1:8
Acts 6:8
1 Corinthians 15:55-57

6

GOD IS CLOSE TO EVERYWHERE

PRESENT EVERYWHERE, OMNIPRESENT

His Nature

Because God is infinite, the words *limit* and *limitation* can never be used to describe his presence in space or time. As A. W. Tozer points out, God "is near to everything and everyone. He is here; He is next to you wherever you may be. And if you send up the furious question, 'Oh God, where art Thou?' the answer comes back, 'I am where you are; I am here; I am next to you; I am close to everywhere.' That's what the Bible says."[1]

God is not contained in the universe, but the universe is contained in God. As Tozer says, "God fills heaven and earth just as the ocean fills a bucket which has been submerged in it a mile down. The bucket is full of the ocean, but the ocean surrounds the bucket in all directions."[2]

Even when we feel abandoned, God is still Immanuel. He is still "God . . . with us" (Isaiah 7:14).

Key Scripture

There [in the Tabernacle] I will meet with you and speak with you. I will meet the people of Israel there, in the place made holy by my glorious presence.

EXODUS 29:42-43

Monday

GOD REVEALS HIMSELF

These burnt offerings are to be made each day from generation to generation. Offer them in the LORD's presence at the Tabernacle entrance; there I will meet with you and speak with you. I will meet the people of Israel there, in the place made holy by my glorious presence. Yes, I will consecrate the Tabernacle and the altar, and I will consecrate Aaron and his sons to serve me as priests. Then I will live among the people of Israel and be their God, and they will know that I am the LORD their God. I am the one who brought them out of the land of Egypt so that I could live among them. I am the LORD their God.

EXODUS 29:42-46

He came into the very world he created, but the world didn't recognize him. He came to his own people, and even they rejected him. But to all who believed him and accepted him, he gave the right to become children of God. They are reborn—not with a physical birth resulting from human passion or plan, but a birth that comes from God.

So the Word became human and made his home among us. He was full of unfailing love and faithfulness. And we have seen his glory, the glory of the Father's one and only Son.

JOHN 1:10-14

Understanding His Presence

The Bible makes it clear that God is everywhere. There isn't one square inch of creation in which he is not present. Yet even though God is omnipresent, he is distinct from the world he has made, existing apart from it. What's more, Scripture tells us that God is present in a special way with his people.

95

Let's briefly trace the story of God's presence from its beginning, when Adam and Eve had unfettered access to God, walking with him in the Garden of Eden. At first there was nothing separating them from him. But it wasn't long until the two were expelled from his presence, separated by their disobedience (Genesis 3:23).

Yet God refused to abandon them. Instead he set a plan in motion to reach out to a people he had formed, teaching them what it means to live in the presence of a holy God.

Even before delivering his people from Egypt, God revealed himself to Moses in the form of a burning bush. Later, as he was rescuing them from the power of Pharaoh, he manifested his presence in a "pillar of cloud" and a "pillar of fire," which led them through the wilderness (Exodus 13:21-22).

Then God manifested his presence in the Tabernacle, which means "tent," "place of dwelling," or "sanctuary." The Bible also refers to it as the "tent of meeting"—a sacred place in which God would meet with representatives of his people (Exodus 33:7). The Tabernacle was a mobile structure with movable furniture designed to accompany them on their journey into the land God promised to give them—a tangible sign of God's presence with them no matter where they went. Later, King Solomon built the Temple in Jerusalem. There in the innermost sanctuary, the "Holy of Holies," or the "Most Holy Place," God's presence would dwell on earth.

The Greek word *skēnoō* can be translated "tabernacled" or "spread tent." It appears in John 1:14, which says that "the Word became flesh and made his dwelling among us" (NIV). In other words, "The Word became flesh and *tabernacled* among us."

The New Testament also speaks of Jesus making his home in the hearts of his people through faith (Ephesians 3:17) and of the indwelling of the Holy Spirit (2 Timothy 1:14).

In addition, the New Testament uses the word *parousia*, which means "coming presence," to refer to Christ's second coming, when his presence within the world will no longer be hidden but be obvious to everyone. When that happens, those who belong to him will receive this promise: "Look, God's home is now among his people! He will live with them, and they will be his people. God himself will be with them. He will wipe every tear from their eyes, and there will be no more death or sorrow or crying or pain. All these things are gone forever" (Revelation 21:3-4).

Lord, thank you for your presence in my life and in the world around me. I pray today that you will increase my spiritual sensitivity, helping me to recognize your presence. Be gracious, Lord. Open my eyes to see your face.

Studying His Presence

1. God calls the Tabernacle "the place made holy by my glorious presence." What are the implications of this passage for our own places of worship, even though they differ from the Tabernacle spoken of in the passage?

2. What must it have felt like for an enslaved people—the lowest of the low—to be delivered through the intervention of a God who was near enough to hear their cries for help and powerful enough to help? How does God's presence deliver us from evil?

3. What does God's desire to dwell among his people say about his character and his intentions regarding us?

4. John's Gospel indicates that when Jesus came into the world he had created, the world failed to recognize him (John 1:10). Why do you think so many people in Jesus' day were blind to the presence of God in their midst?

5. Have you ever been especially aware of God's presence in your own life? If so, what were the circumstances? How did the experience affect you?

Tuesday

PRAYING IN LIGHT OF GOD'S PRESENCE

He came into the very world he created, but the world didn't recognize him. He came to his own people, and even they rejected him.

JOHN 1:10-11

Reflect On: John 1:10-14
Praise God: For wanting to manifest himself to you
Offer Thanks: For God's faithful presence in your life
Confess: Your attachment to things that dull your
    spiritual hunger
Ask God: To increase your longing for his holy presence

This morning I walked down from my attic office and into the kitchen. To my alarm, I realized I wasn't the only one in the house. I heard noises, and then I spotted a garbage bag and a pile of dirt in the middle of the floor—not the usual traces of a burglary in process. Suddenly I remembered that it was Friday, the day our cleaning lady comes to work her wonders.

My experience this morning reminded me that we don't always register the presence of another even when he or she is nearby. And God is always nearby.

John's Gospel says something stunning about God's entrance into the world. It tells us that Jesus "came into the very world he created, but the world didn't recognize him." How could the Creator of the universe slip into the world unnoticed? And how could creatures he made fail to register his presence?

I don't have an answer except to admit how thick we humans can be, how slow to recognize the presence of God in our lives. It causes me to wonder what in my life desensitizes me to his presence. Here's my short list: trouble, busyness, materialism, worry, and sin. Of course, the biggest item on my list is the last one. Sin has a way of dulling my spiritual senses, creating barriers in my relationship with God.

But the real stealth bombers, the dangers most of us are least aware of, are materialism and busyness, because these can easily become a way of life for those who live in cultures that promote such values. As we fill every moment with tasks and train every desire on acquiring material goods (a sin in itself), our spiritual sensibilities wither.

If it's been a while since you experienced God, ask him to increase your spiritual hunger. Pray that he will point out anything that may be an obstacle. Then consider engaging in one of the spiritual disciplines—solitude, silence, prayer, fasting, confession, giving, simplicity, or Bible study—as a way of opening your soul to a deeper awareness of his presence.

Wednesday

PRAYING IN LIGHT OF GOD'S PRESENCE

O LORD, why do you stand so far away?
    Why do you hide when I am in trouble?

PSALM 10:1

Don't hide from your servant;
    answer me quickly, for I am in deep trouble!

PSALM 69:17

O LORD, how long will this go on?
    Will you hide yourself forever?
    How long will your anger burn like fire?

PSALM 89:46

Reflect On:	Psalm 10:1; 69:1-17; 89:46
Praise God:	For his wisdom in revealing himself
Offer Thanks:	For the times when you have felt close to God
Confess:	Any tendency to run away from God when you've done something that displeases him
Ask God:	To reveal himself more deeply to you

If God is close to everywhere, why does he sometimes seem so distant? Is he trying to teach us something, like the lesson my mother was trying to convey to my younger brother when she hid behind the counter at a department store?

When my brother was young, he had a tendency to wander, to be distracted by all the glittering things he saw. But he needed to learn to stay close to her. So she hid. And he cried. And he learned that he had to follow her and that she wasn't going to follow him. Is God waiting for us to learn that too? Is that why he sometimes conceals himself?

Or maybe God hides to increase our hunger for his presence. Jerry Sittser tells a story about playing hide-and-seek with his children. "I was better at hiding than my kids were," he explains. "But I always gave them hints, like little squeaks or hoots, to help them find me. When they discovered my whereabouts, they would squeal with delight because they loved to find me. I never once wanted to hide so well that they would never find me, because the joy of the game came in being found, not in hiding."[5]

Or maybe he hides because he does not want to take unfair advantage. Imagine what might happen if he appeared in Rockefeller Center one day. An amazing, all-powerful, all-knowing God in plain sight. The sheer magnitude of his presence would compel belief. There would be no room for doubt, no need for faith. We would bow down in homage simply because we feared him. But God wants us to love him.

And speaking of hiding, remember how Adam and Eve hid from God when they heard him calling in the Garden? Ashamed of their sin and fearful of consequences, they attempted the impossible—trying to hide from the God who knows everything. Maybe the one who's hiding is not God but us.

Today, as you seek God's presence, open your heart to him. If there is sin, beg forgiveness. If there is dullness, ask for longing. If there is love for God, take that as evidence of his presence. Don't stop seeking. Don't stop praying. Don't stop trusting that God finds joy not in hiding himself but in being found.

Thursday

PRAYING IN LIGHT OF GOD'S PRESENCE

I will reluctantly tell about visions and revelations from the Lord. I was caught up to the third heaven fourteen years ago. Whether I was in my body or out of my body, I don't know—only God knows. Yes, only God knows whether I was in my body or outside my body. But I do know that I was caught up to paradise and heard things so astounding that they cannot be expressed in words, things no human is allowed to tell.

That experience is worth boasting about, but I'm not going to do it. I will boast only about my weaknesses.

2 CORINTHIANS 12:1-5

Reflect On: 2 Corinthians 12:1-5
Praise God: Because his presence is not confined to the physical universe
Offer Thanks: That heaven awaits you
Confess: Your unworthiness to stand in his presence
Ask God: To deepen your relationship with him

Charles Finney was a nineteenth-century evangelist who claimed to have had a remarkable encounter with God. Finney writes

It seemed to me as if I met the Lord Jesus Christ face-to-face. It seemed to me that I saw him as I would see any other man. He said nothing, but looked at me in such a manner as to break me right down at his feet. It seemed to me a reality that he stood before me, and I fell down at his feet and poured out my soul to him. I wept aloud like a child and made such confession as I could with my choked words. It seemed to me that I bathed his feet with my tears, and yet I had no distinct impression that I touched him.

The Holy Spirit descended upon me in a manner that seemed to go through me, body and soul. I could feel the impression, like a wave of electricity, going through and through me. Indeed it seemed to come in waves of liquid love, for I could not express it in any other way. It seemed like the very breath of God. I can remember distinctly that it seemed to fan me, like immense wings.

No words can express the wonderful love that was spread abroad in my heart. I wept aloud with joy and love. I literally bellowed out the unspeakable overflow of my heart. These waves came over me, and over me, and over me, one after another, until I remember crying out, "I shall die if these waves continue to pass over me." I said, "Lord, I cannot bear any more," yet I had no fear of death.[4]

Perhaps you have had an experience of God's presence that has changed your life. If so, thank God for it, and don't let time and circumstances erase the memory. Remember, too, that God reveals himself to people in various ways. We don't all have to be Charles Finneys in order to experience him.

If you want more of God, take a moment to turn to him and recommit your life to him, telling him that you want to submit yourself—your will, your desires, your whole being—to him. Ask for the grace to experience him in whatever way he wants to manifest his presence in your life. Don't seek the experience, but do seek God.

Friday

PROMISES ASSOCIATED WITH GOD'S PRESENCE

One of the greatest promises of the Bible is the last one Jesus gave—after his resurrection and prior to his return to heaven: "Be sure of this," he told his disciples. "I am with you always, even to the end of the age" (Matthew 28:20). Notice that he didn't say, "I'm with you sometimes." Nor did he say, "I'm there most of the time." He said, "I am with you always." So whether you're depressed, angry, confused, hungry, sick, or penniless, Jesus is still with you. No matter what's going on in your life, he is close to you. While it's great to have a friend by your side when life is difficult, it's even better to have someone who is unfazed by the darkness around you. Even in the midst of it, Christ will be your shelter and your joy.

No matter how you're feeling right now, why not enter God's holy presence by singing his praises? Lift up your voice and express your confidence that he is near and that he will show you the way of life.

Promises in Scripture

> You will show me the way of life,
>   granting me the joy of your presence
>   and the pleasures of living with you forever.
>
> PSALM 16:11

> How great is the goodness
>   you have stored up for those who fear you.
> You lavish it on those who come to you for
>   protection,
>   blessing them before the watching world.

You hide them in the shelter of your
    presence,
  safe from those who conspire against
    them.
You shelter them in your presence,
  far from accusing tongues.

PSALM 31:19-20

I can never escape from your Spirit!
  I can never get away from your
    presence!
If I go up to heaven, you are there;
  if I go down to the grave, you are there.
If I ride the wings of the morning,
  if I dwell by the farthest oceans,
even there your hand will guide me,
  and your strength will support me.
I could ask the darkness to hide me
  and the light around me to become
    night—
  but even in darkness I cannot hide
    from you.
To you the night shines as bright as day.
  Darkness and light are the same to you.

PSALM 139:7-12

Teach these new disciples to obey all the commands I have given you.
And be sure of this: I am with you always, even to the end of the age.

MATTHEW 28:20

Because of Christ and our faith in him, we can now come boldly and
confidently into God's presence.

EPHESIANS 3:12

Continued Prayer and Praise

Genesis 28:10-16
2 Chronicles 5:14
Psalm 16:7-10
Psalm 68:2-3
Jeremiah 23:23-24
Acts 3:19-20

7

GOD IS NEVER SURPRISED

ALL KNOWING, OMNISCIENT

His Nature

God is never confused and never perplexed. He doesn't need to study, investigate, explore, find out, or revise his thinking, because he already has perfect knowledge of everything and everyone—including you. If you tried to hide from him or surprise him or shock him or frighten him, you would fail. He never has to wonder what you might be thinking or what you're going to do next, because he already knows. Truly, his knowledge is too wonderful for us.

Key Scripture

You see me when I travel
and when I rest at home.
You know everything I do.
You know what I am going to say
even before I say it, LORD.
You go before me and follow me.
You place your hand of blessing on my head.
Such knowledge is too wonderful for me,
too great for me to understand!

PSALM 139:3-6

Monday

GOD REVEALS HIMSELF

How great is our Lord! His power is absolute!
His understanding is beyond comprehension!

PSALM 147:5

O LORD, you have examined my heart
and know everything about me.
You know when I sit down or stand up.
You know my thoughts even when I'm far away.
You see me when I travel
and when I rest at home.
You know everything I do.
You know what I am going to say
even before I say it, LORD.
You go before me and follow me.
You place your hand of blessing on my head.
Such knowledge is too wonderful for me,
too great for me to understand! . . .

You made all the delicate, inner parts of my body
and knit me together in my mother's womb.
Thank you for making me so wonderfully complex!
Your workmanship is marvelous—how well I
know it.
You watched me as I was being formed in utter
seclusion,
as I was woven together in the dark of the womb.
You saw me before I was born.
Every day of my life was recorded in your book.
Every moment was laid out
before a single day had passed.

How precious are your thoughts about me,
    O God.
They cannot be numbered!
I can't even count them;
    they outnumber the grains of sand!
And when I wake up,
    you are still with me!

PSALM 139:1-6, 13-18

Understanding His Omniscience

Scripture teaches that there is no limit to God's knowledge, no boundary to his understanding. There is never a question he cannot answer or a mystery he cannot fathom. He penetrates the depths of everything and everyone, including us.

If the prospect of an all-seeing, all-knowing God sounds frightening, consider how frightening the alternative would be. What if God were all powerful but not all knowing? Like a bull in a china shop, an all-powerful god with limited understanding could inflict terrible damage with one simple mistake. He could commit horrible injustices—not because of ill will, but because he didn't have all the facts. Even if he were right most of the time, he would still be a bumbler some of the time. How could you rely on him and trust in his promises? A less-than-omniscient god would be a less-than-perfect god, capable of creating enormous havoc by virtue of his limited understanding.

Fortunately, as Scripture tells us, there is not the slightest defect in God's knowledge. For those who belong to him, God's perfect understanding of the past, the present, and the future is a source of great confidence. It means that he knows what he's doing and that he's able to fulfill his plans and purposes. It also means that he will never misunderstand us and that he will always act justly.

The Hebrew verb *ya⁻da'* is translated "to know." It can apply to knowledge that is gained primarily through sensory experience as well as knowledge that comes through the intellect. At times the word *yada* describes the relationship of two people in a covenant. To know the Lord means to acknowledge the covenant relationship. Similarly, yada can express the sexual relationship between husband and wife, as in Genesis 4:1, which says that "Adam knew Eve his wife; and she conceived" (KJV).

The Hebrew word *da'at* is derived from the verb *yada*. It means knowledge in every aspect of life, including the moral aspect. This word is found in Genesis 2:9, which says, "In the middle of the garden [God] placed the tree of life and the tree of the knowledge [*da'at*] of good and evil." Our knowledge is always partial, while God's knowledge is always complete. To be able to make important moral distinctions, we need to rely not on our feelings or instincts, but on what God has taught us about right and wrong.

The Bible makes it clear that knowledge comes from God: "Fear of the LORD is the foundation of true knowledge" (Proverbs 1:7). Even though some people may be considered brilliant by the world's standards, their knowledge is of little value if they refuse to acknowledge God, the source of all wisdom. Psalm 14:1 says it plainly: "Only fools say in their hearts, 'There is no God.'"

Those who flaunt God will find the thought of an omniscient God unsettling, while those who love him will take comfort in knowing he has ordered each of their days.

Lord, you possess not only all power but also all knowledge.
Nothing is hidden from you. Increase my fear of you, my sense
of awe in knowing who you are. As I seek the understanding
only you can give, help me to follow you with trust and
obedience.

Studying His Omniscience

1. How does it make you feel when you realize that God knows everything?

2. David, the author of Psalm 139, seems to have been given a profound understanding of God's omniscience. How and why might God have communicated this to him?

3. Have you ever had a sense that God knew everything about you? What were the circumstances?

4. Have you ever felt the need to explain yourself to God? Have you ever felt misunderstood by him? If so, what happened?

5. Why is it important to know, as David proclaims, that God sees us before we are born and that he has recorded every one of our days in his book?

6. How might your perspective change if you lived every day with a profound awareness of God's omniscience?

Tuesday

PRAYING IN LIGHT OF GOD'S OMNISCIENCE

When they arrived at the place where God had told him to go, Abraham built an altar and arranged the wood on it. Then he tied his son, Isaac, and laid him on the altar on top of the wood. And Abraham picked up the knife to kill his son as a sacrifice. At that moment the angel of the LORD called to him from heaven, "Abraham! Abraham!"

"Yes," Abraham replied. "Here I am!"

"Don't lay a hand on the boy!" the angel said. "Do not hurt him in any way, for now I know that you truly fear God. You have not withheld from me even your son, your only son."

Then Abraham looked up and saw a ram caught by its horns in a thicket. So he took the ram and sacrificed it as a burnt offering in place of his son. Abraham named the place Yahweh-Yireh (which means "the LORD will provide"). To this day, people still use that name as a proverb: "On the mountain of the LORD it will be provided."

GENESIS 22:9-14

Reflect On: Genesis 22:9-14

Praise God: For providing for our needs, which he sees
             in advance

Offer Thanks: For the provision of God's forgiveness and
             love

Confess: Any tendency to wallow in guilt, believing
             that God cannot forgive you

Ask God: To help you lean into the salvation his Son
             has won for you

When people use the phrase "fall down laughing," they don't usually mean it literally. But that's precisely what I did many years ago when my older brother and I were fooling around with friends, chasing each other around the outside of the house one afternoon. I was in middle school at the time, and he was in high school. I was in hot pursuit when I suddenly reversed course, hoping to catch him as he rounded the side of the house. As soon as I turned the corner, I realized we were running full speed directly at each other. Before I could shout, "Gotcha!" Bob fell down. Actually, both of us did: he collapsed in surprise, and I fell over laughing.

Surprises can be delightful—as when we hear from an old friend we've lost contact with or receive a gift we cherish. But they can be painful, too, when they take the shape of a sudden betrayal, an unexpected loss, or a surprise attack.

When unpleasant situations sneak up on us, we can draw comfort from the fact that God is never surprised by the things that throw us into turmoil. One of God's titles is *Yahweh-Yireh*, which is translated "the LORD will provide." The English word *provision* (pro-vision) is made up of two Latin words meaning "to see beforehand." Similarly, *yireh* is derived from the Hebrew word *rā'â*, which means "to see." Since God sees the future, as well as the past and the present, he is uniquely able to provide what we need to deal with the troubles that assail us.

The name Yahweh-Yireh appears in the book of Genesis, most notably in the story of Abraham and Isaac. When Abraham was about to sacrifice his son in obedience to God, an angel suddenly appeared and saved Isaac's life. Catching sight of a ram caught in a thicket, Abraham sacrificed the animal instead—a sacrifice that prefigured the sacrifice of Jesus on the cross. Tellingly,

Scripture says that "Abraham named the place Yahweh-Yireh (which means 'the LORD will provide')" (Genesis 22:14). God knew exactly what Abraham and Isaac needed, and he knows what we need as well.

Once we grasp the truth that God is never taken by surprise, we should no longer fall into the trap of chronic guilt. Guilt that leads to repentance and forgiveness is good, but chronic guilt cripples our sense of God's love.

Think of the worst sin you have ever committed, whether before or after giving your life to Christ. The Lord knew exactly how you would fail in that moment, but he loved you anyway. He loved you so much that he sent his Son to save you. And that's how much he loves you now.

Wednesday

PRAYING IN LIGHT OF GOD'S OMNISCIENCE

Nothing in all creation is hidden from God. Everything is naked and exposed before his eyes, and he is the one to whom we are accountable.

So then, since we have a great High Priest who has entered heaven, Jesus the Son of God, let us hold firmly to what we believe. This High Priest of ours understands our weaknesses, for he faced all of the same testings we do, yet he did not sin. So let us come boldly to the throne of our gracious God. There we will receive his mercy, and we will find grace to help us when we need it most.

HEBREWS 4:13-16

Reflect On:	Hebrews 4:13-16
Praise God:	Because he understands everything, including our weaknesses
Offer Thanks:	Because Christ experienced every test we face
Confess:	Any doubts about God's mercy
Ask God:	To enable you to ask for his help and expect it to come

Do you know that sneezes can travel as fast as one hundred miles per hour? Or that 111,111,111 x 111,111,111 = 12,345,678,987,654,321? Or that you can make dynamite using peanuts? Or how about some big-time questions, like the ones God asked Job? Do you know the path to the source of light or where the home of the east wind is? Do you know how to direct the movement of the stars or the sequence of the seasons? Can you catch a crocodile with a hook and make it a pet like a bird or give it to your children to play with?

If you don't know the answer to every question in the universe, from the most trivial detail to the greatest mystery of the universe, relax. It just means you're not God.

How can we begin to understand a being for whom there is no such thing as mystery, ambiguity, or misunderstanding? A God who never needs to learn anything and from whom nothing is hidden? A God incapable of experiencing even a sliver of doubt or a moment of confusion?

As remarkable as God's knowledge is, it is also remarkable to realize how intimately he knows us. Listen to what the book of Hebrews says about Jesus: "This High Priest of ours understands our weaknesses" (4:15). If God is omniscient—if he knows everything—then there has never been a time when he didn't know who we are and what we are made of. There has never been a moment in which he failed to sympathize with our struggles as human beings.

Paul tells the Philippians that Jesus "emptied himself, taking the form of a servant, being born in the likeness of men" (2:7, RSV). By becoming one of us, Jesus took things a step further, assuring us that his knowledge of the human condition is concrete, not theoretical. His knowledge is intimate, caring, complete.

That knowledge, of course, extends to those around us as well—including those we are most tempted to judge. Let's resist the slide toward self-righteousness by reminding ourselves that God is the only one who knows enough to judge anyone's heart.

Thursday

PRAYING IN LIGHT OF GOD'S OMNISCIENCE

O LORD, *you have examined my heart*
and know everything about me.
You know when I sit down or stand up.
You know my thoughts even when
I'm far away.
You see me when I travel
and when I rest at home.
You know everything I do.
You know what I am going to say
even before I say it, LORD.
You go before me and follow me.
You place your hand of blessing
on my head.
Such knowledge is too wonderful for me,
too great for me to understand! . . .

You made all the delicate, inner parts of my body
and knit me together in my mother's womb.
Thank you for making me so wonderfully complex!
Your workmanship is marvelous—how well I
know it.
You watched me as I was being formed in utter
seclusion,
as I was woven together in the dark of
the womb.
You saw me before I was born.
Every day of my life was recorded in
your book.
Every moment was laid out
before a single day had passed.

How precious are your thoughts about me,
    O God.
  They cannot be numbered!
I can't even count them;
    they outnumber the grains of sand!
And when I wake up,
    you are still with me!

PSALM 139:1-6, 13-18

Reflect On: Psalm 139:1-6, 13-18
Praise God: Because his understanding is complete
Offer Thanks: Because God has recorded every day of your life
    in his book
Confess: Any tendency to let worry control you
Ask God: To help you rest in the fact that God knows you
    and knows how to take care of you

I felt it the other day—that pang of worry cutting through my gut.

My first thought was to analyze the problem, turning it over and over in my mind, as though it were a hunk of meat roasting endlessly on a spit. But that approach has never worked for me. Instead, something obvious occurred to me. *Wait a minute—I tell other people that worry is nothing but a negative use of the imagination. Maybe I should follow my own advice and ask God for help.* So I did. I thought about the matter and then offered up a brief prayer. Before I knew it, my anxiety had vanished.

But it doesn't always work like that. Sometimes our worries are so strong they send us headlong into a sea of fear, with the result that we begin uttering what I call "worry prayers." This brand of praying may be better than no prayer at all, but not much. Why? Because it simply puts a spiritual facade on our worries. Here's how such a "prayer" might sound: "Lord, help! My husband lost his job. When that happened last time, he got so depressed. We could hardly pay our bills. Now he's older—it's going to be impossible for him to find work if he's depressed. And my job isn't going well either. What if I get fired? What are we going to do?" And on and on we go, with never a pause to hear God's voice and receive his help.

What if we began our prayers by doing something counter-intuitive? Instead of focusing on our concerns, we could focus on God—on his omniscience, power, and faithfulness. We could do this by recalling specific ways God has helped us in the past or by reading stories and passages from the Bible that display his faithfulness in the midst of difficult circumstances. We could spend time thanking and praising him.

Worry is a contagion that can spread quickly from one human being to the next. But it can never spread from us to God because God never worries. Instead, the reverse can happen. His calm can come to characterize our lives as we learn to enter his presence and lean on his understanding rather than our own.

The next time you're tempted to let worry control you, don't take the easy path by giving in to it. As you turn to God, resist the temptation to explain everything that's wrong to a God who already knows what you're facing. Be honest about what's troubling you, but don't get stuck there. Turn to God so he can be gracious to you.

Friday

PROMISES ASSOCIATED WITH GOD'S OMNISCIENCE

Psalm 103 paints a particular picture of God. The psalmist doesn't say that God is some kind of aloof, celestial headmaster expecting five-year-olds to master trigonometry. Nor does he depict God as an unreasonable boss, pressuring his employees to accomplish impossible goals. No, the metaphor the psalmist employs is intimate and familiar. He draws a picture of God as an affectionate Father whose knowledge of his children's weakness elicits tenderness and compassion.

This psalmist knows that God is never surprised by our failures. He never goes into a rage when we sin, and he never judges us simply because our emotions don't align with his truths. Though God calls us to grow into his likeness, and though he is delighted as we do, he knows we will struggle toward that goal. Like any good father, he loves us in the midst of our struggles. Our call as Christians is not to try to please an unforgiving God but to trust in God's fatherly care, leaning into his compassion and relying on his kindness even as we struggle to be more like him.

Promises in Scripture

> The LORD is like a father to his children,
>   tender and compassionate to those
>   who fear him.
> For he knows how weak we are;
>   he remembers we are only dust.

PSALM 103:13-14

The very hairs on your head are all numbered.

MATTHEW 10:30

123

Our actions will show that we belong to the truth, so we will be confident when we stand before God. Even if we feel guilty, God is greater than our feelings, and he knows everything.

1 JOHN 3:19-20

Continued Prayer and Praise
1 Samuel 2:3
Job 28:23-28
Psalm 147:5
Proverbs 15:11
Isaiah 40:12-14
Isaiah 46:9-10
Isaiah 55:8-9
John 21:17
Hebrews 4:13

8

GOD IS NEVER FRUSTRATED

PATIENT

His Nature

One way to understand God's patience is by considering the greatness of his power. As Charles Spurgeon once observed, those with truly great power also possess the power to control themselves. God has the power, then, to curb his own power, to restrain his anger for a higher good. As Spurgeon puts it, "The power that binds omnipotence is omnipotence surpassed."[1] God's strength is what enables him to bear insults and offenses without immediately punishing those who commit them. So patience is a virtue based on strength, not weakness. God's patience is borne out of his desire to welcome all into his Kingdom, allowing each of us the chance to repent and receive his forgiveness.

Key Scripture

I am slow to anger
and filled with unfailing love and faithfulness.

EXODUS 34:6

Monday

GOD REVEALS HIMSELF

"I will remove my hand and let you see me from behind. But my face will not be seen."

Then the LORD told Moses, "Chisel out two stone tablets like the first ones. I will write on them the same words that were on the tablets you smashed. Be ready in the morning to climb up Mount Sinai and present yourself to me on the top of the mountain. No one else may come with you. In fact, no one is to appear anywhere on the mountain. Do not even let the flocks or herds graze near the mountain."

So Moses chiseled out two tablets of stone like the first ones. Early in the morning he climbed Mount Sinai as the LORD had commanded him, and he carried the two stone tablets in his hands.

Then the LORD came down in a cloud and stood there with him; and he called out his own name, Yahweh. The LORD passed in front of Moses, calling out,

> "Yahweh! The LORD!
>   The God of compassion and mercy!
> I am slow to anger
>   and filled with unfailing love and faithfulness."

EXODUS 33:23–34:6

Understanding His Patience

The Hebrew phrase *'erek 'appayim* is translated "patient," "long-suffering," or "slow to anger." Usually used in Scripture to refer to God, the phrase characterizes one who is wise, a peacemaker. A person who excels in this quality may even have the ability to persuade the powerful. Proverbs 25:15 says that "patience can persuade a prince, and soft speech can break bones."

In the New Testament, the Greek verb *makrothymeō* and the noun *makrothymiea* are usually translated as some form of "patient endurance." According to one Bible dictionary, the words come from the root words for "long" and "soul," indicating "to be long of feeling, delay one's anger."[2] God is calling us to be long or large in spirit, willing to exercise faith while we wait for him to act. Like Abraham, we need to exercise patience when it comes to waiting for God's promises (Hebrews 6:15), and we need patience in awaiting Christ's return (James 5:7-8).

To those who ask why God allows the wicked to go unpunished, God indicates that justice will eventually be done. Meanwhile, he wants as many people as possible to repent and come into his Kingdom. Just as the Lord has been patient with us, we are called to be patient with others.

Patience is not primarily a matter of temperament but rather a fruit of the Spirit (Galatians 5:22). Exercising patience takes courage and faith, without which waiting can become unbearable. God will grow this fruit in us as we wait upon him, increasing our wisdom and enabling us to do his will and reflect his character to others.

Lord, let your Spirit bring forth the fruit of patience in my life. Give me the grace to turn to you first and not last so that anxiety and frustration won't push me into reacting to life in ungodly ways.

Studying His Patience

1. How has God shown patience toward you? Be as specific as possible.
2. The scene described in Exodus 34:5-7 occurred immediately after God inscribed the Ten Commandments on two stone tablets. Comment on the significance of this timing.

3. On a scale of 1 to 10, with 10 being the highest, how would you rate your ability to be patient? What could you do to improve your score?
4. Why is it hard to be patient?
5. Do you ever think God gets frustrated with you? Why or why not?

Tuesday

PRAYING IN LIGHT OF GOD'S PATIENCE

> *Yahweh! The LORD!*
> *The God of compassion and mercy!*
> *I am slow to anger*
> *and filled with unfailing love and faithfulness.*

EXODUS 34:6

Reflect On: Exodus 34:6

Praise God: For the slowness of his anger

Offer Thanks: That God is not quick to punish

Confess: Any tendency toward impatience and uncontrolled anger

Ask God: To teach you the meaning of patience

During the first semester of my freshman year in college, I was required to take a natural-science course. In one class the professor asked the students to measure their noses. Though I don't remember the point of this unusual exercise, which might have been about understanding terms like *mean, mode,* and *average,* I do remember that I was the proud possessor of the shortest nose in the class.

Though I haven't thought of that incident for many years, the memory returned once I began studying the biblical meaning of the Hebrew idiom for patience, which can also be translated as "long-suffering" or "slow to anger." The phrase *'erek 'appayim* literally means "long of nose." Armed with that information, you now realize that Exodus 34:6 could be translated like this:

Yahweh! The LORD!
  The God of compassion and mercy!
I am long of nose
  and filled with unfailing love and faithfulness.

In English, having a long nose means you have a habit of lying. But in Hebrew, it means you have a habit of being patient. Though God's nature is to be patient, he can be provoked. Consider Psalm 18:8, which depicts God's anger this way: "Smoke poured from his nostrils." The psalmist evokes the image of flared nostrils and a nose that's red with rage. Because God is slow to anger, it takes a long time for his nose to get red.

According to Proverbs, having a long nose is associated with wisdom and great understanding. It also enables the wise person to calm those who are quarreling. By contrast, those who are qebar 'appayim, "short of nose," are quick tempered and impatient. They are hotheads and fools.

The next time you feel your face flushing scarlet or your nose turning red, remember the phrase "long of nose." Allow yourself to enjoy the humor of that image. It may prevent you from becoming impatient and doing something foolish. Remember also that frustration, irritation, annoyance, and anger are not God's default setting. Patience is. When he looks at you and others, his heart is filled with so much love and faithfulness that he is always erek appayim.

Wednesday

PRAYING IN LIGHT OF GOD'S PATIENCE

The Lord isn't really being slow about his promise, as some people think. No, he is being patient for your sake. He does not want anyone to be destroyed, but wants everyone to repent. But the day of the Lord will come as unexpectedly as a thief. Then the heavens will pass away with a terrible noise, and the very elements themselves will disappear in fire, and the earth and everything on it will be found to deserve judgment.

2 PETER 3:9-10

Reflect On: 2 Peter 3:9-10
Praise God: For delaying judgment so more people will have
                 a chance to repent
Offer Thanks: For the ways God has been patient with you
Confess: Any rush to judgment in your own heart
Ask God: To show you the difference between patience
                 and indulgence

I am a believer in allowing adults to get to the end of their rope when they insist on pursuing a self-destructive course. Though it can be frightening to watch those we love unravel as they pursue a foolish path, we can pray that it will eventually create the space for God to work.

That was the pattern in my own life. As a college student, I was swallowed up in a relativistic culture whose slogan was "If it feels good, do it." It wasn't long before I became immersed in the drug culture, and my life began to fall to pieces. It took a few years, but by the grace of God, I came to a place where I realized my only hope was Christ. God knew the precise moment I would face the graveness of my situation, tasting the bitterness of sin and calling it what it was. There, in the midst of near hopelessness, he extended his grace and saved me. Looking back, I see how patient he was, always pursuing and never giving up on me.

What if he had not been patient? What if he had simply struck me down and punished me as I deserved? What if he'd called me out for a fool and then destroyed me? Then he would not be the God I have come to know. He would not be the lover of my soul or the lifter of my head. He wouldn't be so many of the things we sing about. But glory to God, he is all those things and more.

Today as you think about the Lord, who is slow to anger and who postpones judgment, consider all the ways he has shown patience with you. Praise him and ask him for the grace to display his patience to others.

Thursday

PRAYING IN LIGHT OF GOD'S PATIENCE

Wait patiently for the LORD.
  Be brave and courageous.
  Yes, wait patiently for the LORD.

PSALM 27:14

Be still in the presence of the LORD,
  and wait patiently for him to act.
Don't worry about evil people who prosper
  or fret about their wicked schemes.

PSALM 37:7

Reflect On: Psalm 27:14; Psalm 37:7
Praise God: For giving us his Spirit, who can help us grow
        in patience
Offer Thanks: For the ways God has already worked in your
        times of waiting
Confess: Any tendency to try to control outcomes
Ask God: To increase your faith as you wait

I'm not a good waiter. I don't mean the kind that works in a restaurant (though I wouldn't be good at that, either). I'm talking about the fact that I dislike waiting for anything. That's why I'm rarely early, because I don't like waiting around. I haven't the patience.

Waiting is boring and painful. It's not for busy people like me. Except that it is, because I'm human, and human beings have to wait at times. I'm also a human being who belongs to God, and God often commends us for waiting.

As a not-very-good waiter, at least I'm in good company. Look at Job's chutzpah in asking this question: "Why must the godly wait for [God] in vain?" (24:1). Job wanted to know why God allowed the wicked to prevail. And what about the author of the longest psalm in the Bible? This man couldn't stop praising God for the perfection of God's law. Yet neither could he keep himself from lamenting God's apparent slowness in bringing justice to lawbreakers, exclaiming, "How long must I wait?" (Psalm 119:84). Surely waiting for justice must be one of the hardest kinds of waiting a person will ever have to do.

And then there are times when we have to wait for a promise to be fulfilled or a prayer to be answered. Waiting is hard because it exposes our weakness, our inability to control things. We think we know what's best, but we haven't the power to make the "best" happen. Or we dislike the feeling that comes when problems aren't resolved. We want closure. Forced to wait, we do it reluctantly, praying and churning with worry.

Sometimes wisdom requires that we act and act decisively. But when waiting is called for, how should we conduct ourselves? The Bible suggests that our times of waiting should be active, not passive. Passive waiting is like going to the gym and just sitting around, hoping to get stronger without doing shoulder presses, lateral raises, or crunches. Just as we should be in a little better shape when we walk out of a gym, times of waiting should make us stronger because we have been exercising whatever patience, faith, and courage we already have. Waiting on God should also improve our ability to hear his voice, because we have made space in ourselves to actively listen.

I'm still not an accomplished waiter, but I think my skills have improved over the years. Though my natural tendency is toward action, God has helped me realize that often I need to wait to act until I have the wisdom to act well. Experience has also taught me to avoid making hard-and-fast plans about the future, because the future keeps surprising me. Since I can recognize God's faithfulness in the past, I can more peacefully wait for his guidance in the present. Even my failures have been valuable because I've learned how foolish it is to let fear and desire drive my decisions rather than waiting patiently for God's guidance.

What are you waiting for today? Instead of giving in to frustration and impatience, why not ask God to help you use this time as a spiritual workout, helping you to cooperate with his Spirit so you will come out stronger, not weaker?

Friday

PROMISES ASSOCIATED WITH GOD'S PATIENCE

God has made wonderful promises to those who love him. But many of his promises depend on our willingness to trust him enough to do his will. Think of it like this: if you want to build a healthy retirement account, you have to defer spending now so you will have money later. Patient endurance is like invested capital. As we keep living in obedience to God, aligning ourselves to his Word regardless of the challenges, God will do what he has promised, making our lives rich beyond measure.

Just as saving money requires self-discipline, so does patience. We need to forsake our tendency to trust ourselves more than we trust God, restraining our impulse to give in to fear and the desire for temporary pleasures. By patiently enduring testing and temptation, we will one day receive a crown of life.

Promises in Scripture

> *Return to the LORD your God,*
> *for he is merciful and compassionate,*
> *slow to get angry and filled with unfailing*
> *love.*
> *He is eager to relent and not punish.*

JOEL 2:13

The Holy Spirit produces this kind of fruit in our lives: love, joy, peace, patience, kindness, goodness, faithfulness, gentleness, and self-control.

GALATIANS 5:22-23

Patient endurance is what you need now, so that you will continue to do God's will. Then you will receive all that he has promised.

HEBREWS 10:36

God blesses those who patiently endure testing and temptation. Afterward they will receive the crown of life that God has promised to those who love him.

JAMES 1:12

Remember, our Lord's patience gives people time to be saved.

2 PETER 3:15

Continued Prayer and Praise

Psalm 37:7-9
Psalm 40:1
Psalm 86:15
Isaiah 40:31
Romans 15:4-5
1 Corinthians 13:4
Revelation 14:12

9

GOD ALWAYS KNOWS WHAT TO DO

WISE

His Nature

God is never at a loss. He's not puzzled, baffled, bewildered, or confused about anything. He doesn't need time to think things over or do more research or consider other opinions before making a decision. He never has to correct course, retract a statement, or apologize for mistakes he has made. God is infinitely wise, able to see the end from the beginning, and he always knows exactly what to do. No problem can stump him. No difficulty can defeat him. Because God is infinitely loving, powerful, and wise, we can trust him.

Key Scripture

> My child, listen to what I say,
>> and treasure my commands.
> Tune your ears to wisdom,
>> and concentrate on understanding.
> Cry out for insight,
>> and ask for understanding.
> Search for them as you would for silver;
>> seek them like hidden treasures.

PROVERBS 2:1-4

Monday

GOD REVEALS HIMSELF

My child, listen to what I say,
and treasure my commands.
Tune your ears to wisdom,
and concentrate on understanding.
Cry out for insight,
and ask for understanding.
Search for them as you would for silver;
seek them like hidden treasures.
Then you will understand what it means
to fear the LORD,
and you will gain knowledge of God.
For the LORD grants wisdom!
From his mouth come knowledge and
understanding.
He grants a treasure of common sense to the
honest.
He is a shield to those who walk with integrity.
He guards the paths of the just
and protects those who are faithful to him.

Then you will understand what is right, just,
and fair,
and you will find the right way to go.
For wisdom will enter your heart,
and knowledge will fill you with joy.
Wise choices will watch over you.
Understanding will keep you safe.

PROVERBS 2:1-11

Understanding His Wisdom

The most common Hebrew word for wisdom in the Old Testament is *hokmâ*, which can be translated "wisdom," "skill," "learning," or "ability." It usually refers to intellectual understanding, though it can also be used for practical skill or aptitude. A wise person is someone who displays a level of mastery in life and who is able to discern the best course of action in a given situation.

Two figures in the Hebrew Scriptures exemplify exceptional wisdom. The first is David's son Solomon. One night Solomon had a dream in which God asked him to name anything he wanted. Instead of requesting fabulous riches or invincible power, Solomon asked for wisdom. And God gladly supplied it, saying he would give the king "a wise and understanding heart such as no one else has had or ever will have!" (1 Kings 3:12).

The second is a figure who appears in the book of Proverbs—a collection of sayings centered on the theme of wisdom, both moral and practical. The hero of this book is a woman—the personification of wisdom depicted in Proverbs 8, who represents God's wisdom and even God himself. Those who follow her advice will find treasure, success, strength, peace, prosperity, and a long life. The villain of Proverbs is her polar opposite—the woman of folly. Falling prey to her enticements leads one in the direction of poverty and destruction.

According to Jeremiah, forsaking God's Word inevitably leads to foolishness and ruin (8:8-9). Deuteronomy says that wisdom comes from doing the will of God (4:6). Both Psalms and Proverbs indicate that fear of the Lord is the foundation of wisdom (Psalm 111:10; Proverbs 1:7).

The New Testament connects wisdom with the Holy Spirit (1 Corinthians 2:1-16) and contrasts it with worldly wisdom, saying, "The message of the cross is foolish to those who are headed for destruction! But we who are being saved know it is the very power of God. As the Scriptures say, 'I will destroy the wisdom of the wise and discard the intelligence of the intelligent'" (1 Corinthians 1:18-19). Jesus is the embodiment of God's wisdom.

The Greek word for wisdom in the New Testament is *sophia*, a word that implies not merely understanding but also acting in complete accordance with that understanding.

A. W. Tozer defines God's wisdom this way: "Wisdom, among other things, is the ability to devise perfect ends and to achieve those ends by the most perfect means. It sees the end from the beginning, so there can be no need to guess or conjecture. Wisdom sees everything in focus, each in proper relation to all, and is thus able to work toward predestined goals with flawless precision."[1]

Though none of us can measure up to this divine standard, we can access God's wisdom by means of Scripture and the Holy Spirit. We grow in wisdom as we forsake our desire to control things and instead trust in God, who alone can always achieve the most perfect ends by the most perfect means.

Lord, help me to love the wisdom that only you can give. When I am headed down a foolish path, correct me. Help me to actively seek and receive the wisdom you provide instead of leaning on my own understanding.

Studying His Wisdom

1. Read the first five sentences in Proverbs 2 and note all the verbs. What do these indicate about how a person can grow in wisdom?
2. According to Proverbs 2, what are some of the benefits of wisdom?
3. When was the last time you failed to act wisely? What were the circumstances, and what were the consequences?

4. Describe a time God gave you wisdom to deal with a particular circumstance. What was the outcome?

5. Why do you think there is such a close relationship between obedience and wisdom?

Tuesday

PRAYING IN LIGHT OF GOD'S WISDOM

Listen as Wisdom calls out!
Hear as understanding raises her voice! . . .
"My words are plain to anyone with
understanding,
clear to those with knowledge.
Choose my instruction rather than silver,
and knowledge rather than pure gold.
For wisdom is far more valuable than rubies.
Nothing you desire can compare
with it. . . .

"And so, my children, listen to me,
for all who follow my ways are joyful.
Listen to my instruction and be wise.
Don't ignore it.
Joyful are those who listen to me,
watching for me daily at my gates,
waiting for me outside my home!
For whoever finds me finds life
and receives favor from the LORD.
But those who miss me injure themselves.
All who hate me love death."

PROVERBS 8:1, 9-11, 32-36

Reflect On: Proverbs 8
Praise God: For his infinite wisdom
Offer Thanks: Because his Word is clear

149

Confess: Any tendency to think you know better
than God
Ask God: To increase your determination to live by his
wisdom

◯

"You dare not run your own life."[2] This warning comes from A. W. Tozer, who is speaking of our tendency to want to be the bosses of our lives. How we deal with this inclination toward taking control, he says, will make the vital difference between whether we fulfill God's plan for our lives and whether we will experience revival or a dead church.

If we want to grow in God's wisdom, the hard truth is that we can't do it without obeying him. Why would God continue to reveal his will to us if we continue to refuse to do it? Rejecting God's guidance not only leads to a heap of trouble, but it also prevents us from experiencing the joy that can come from watching God's plans unfold in the midst of our obedience.

A few months ago I was wrestling with a decision about how to respond to a small ministry I had previously supported, one that was having obvious difficulties. I knew the people in leadership and thought I might be able to influence them even though I didn't sense much openness. So I asked for wisdom and felt God giving it. I was to take a hands-off approach, because God was going to deal with matters himself. But serious problems persisted. So I asked again, "Lord, what should I do? I see structural problems that are being ignored, ones that will jeopardize the ministry's future. If it collapses, people will get hurt."

In the midst of one of these times of prayer, I was in my car, stopped at the intersection of a busy road and a divided highway.

Though I'd driven that way many times, I noticed with special clarity a set of signs and arrows staring me in the face. Here's how the westbound intersection was marked:

I had been asking for God's guidance and it seemed as though he was giving it—in spades. *Don't change direction. Hold to the course I've set. Remember what I told you.*

Though my prayers for guidance aren't always answered so obviously, this one was. Perhaps God spoke so clearly in that instance because he knows how easy it is for me to fall back into thinking I can fix things. My certainty that I know best might well make things worse.

Sometimes we think it's hard to find God's will. But if we're faithfully following Christ, we can trust that God will always tell us what we need to know when we need to know it. For those whose hearts are fixed on God, prayers for wisdom do not go unheeded.

Wednesday

PRAYING IN LIGHT OF GOD'S WISDOM

Though our bodies are dying, our spirits are being renewed every day. For our present troubles are small and won't last very long. Yet they produce for us a glory that vastly outweighs them and will last forever! So we don't look at the troubles we can see now; rather, we fix our gaze on things that cannot be seen. For the things we see now will soon be gone, but the things we cannot see will last forever.

2 CORINTHIANS 4:16-18

*Teach us to realize the brevity of life,
so that we may grow in wisdom.*

PSALM 90:12

Reflect On: 2 Corinthians 4:16-18; Psalm 90:12
Praise God: For his everlasting wisdom
Offer Thanks: Because God makes decisions for your eternal good
Confess: Any tendency to blame God when things don't turn out as you wish
Ask God: To increase your hope of heaven

God's wisdom is immeasurable. It has no height, no depth, no beginning, and no end. He can untangle every problem and piece together every mystery. Because he is infinite, there is nothing his wisdom cannot penetrate. That means that you can never be in a place where God is unable to help you—unless, of course, you choose to reject his help.

Because we humans are subject to time, we usually operate with a short-term perspective, seeking quick answers to pressing problems. Unable to envision the future from God's point of view, we want what we want right now. We are like the twenty-year-old who won't invest in a retirement fund because he can't imagine ever being old enough to need one. The problem with a short-term perspective is that it tips us toward confusion and depression when things don't turn out as we think they should.

But God always keeps eternity in mind. Without an eternal perspective, how could he have sent his Son to die for us? If we want his wisdom to characterize our lives, we need to pray that God will help us to embrace an eternal view of life.

Here's one man who made that shift, as is evident from this letter he sent to friends after getting a terminal diagnosis from his doctor:

Dear Friends,

It's been a while since we wrote, and many of you have asked for an update. I will try to be informative but not too descriptive!

Back in August I had surgery on my head to remove a very large, infected scab due to continued bleeding from my vascular cancer. This necessary surgery left a large wound that bleeds continually and one that the doctors say will not heal due to tumors growing in that area. Thus I sport a very large turban-like wrapped head that my wife gets to dress a few times a day in the most fashionable way.

Last week, after a short bout with painful breathing, it was discovered that I have lesions on my lungs. They are most likely more cancer. So we are now at a crossroads. We have decided against further treatment or surgery and have opted for palliative care.

These last few weeks our friends have showered us with love, soup, flowers, e-mails, meals, cards, visits, phone calls, and prayers that have encouraged and lifted us. It reminds us of our favorite quote from Dr. V. Raymond Edman: "Say not my soul, 'From whence can God relieve my care?' Remember that Omnipotence hath servants everywhere!"

Many of you told us you were praying for us faithfully, and we thank you. God has given us a heart of peace and thanksgiving for so many years of His blessings. Just today we read Psalm 139, and verses 16-17 reminded us, "All the days ordained for me were written in your book before one of them came to be. How precious to me are your thoughts, O God!"

This is a new journey for us, and we wish to travel it in faith and trust in a sovereign God who has already planned each day. Will you pray that with us?

Thank you for your friendship.

Still in His grip,

Tedd and Ruth Bryson

Tedd died a few weeks after that letter was sent. He and his wife, Ruth, had learned the secret of wisdom, relying on the sovereign God who planned every one of their days from the present into eternity.

Thursday

PRAYING IN LIGHT OF GOD'S WISDOM

Tune your ears to wisdom,
and concentrate on understanding.
Cry out for insight,
and ask for understanding.
Search for them as you would for silver;
seek them like hidden treasures.
Then you will understand what it means
to fear the LORD,
and you will gain knowledge of God.
For the LORD grants wisdom!
From his mouth come knowledge and understanding.

PROVERBS 2:2-6

Reflect On: Proverbs 2:2-6
Praise God: For sharing his wisdom with you
Offer Thanks: For his guidance
Confess: Any tendency to act before thinking
(and praying)
Ask God: To increase your wisdom

I offended someone this morning. My sin consisted of forwarding an article regarding an important moral issue that had recently spurred controversy in the news.

Normally I refrain from such behavior because I get as annoyed as anyone else by e-mails spouting political opinions. But this

155

time the matter seemed of critical importance, and I sent the message without thinking it through.

One of the relatives I'd sent it to reacted as though he'd been stung by killer bees, scolding me for sending an article that directly contradicted his views. I don't blame him. He probably thought I was judging him and trying to persuade him to change his mind. (I admit to the latter offense.)

As I thought about the issue, I concluded I'd made a mistake. I was wrong to have sent the article without first praying for wisdom, especially since I knew it was likely to provoke a negative reaction. I had merely acted on instinct, too busy to take the time to wait for God's guidance. And that was unwise.

Fortunately I'm not always so clueless. Not long ago, I was seeking God for wisdom regarding one of my children who's not particularly good at letting me know about homework assignments, special projects, or school events. I had tried to talk to her about the issue, but nothing changed. The answer to my prayer for wisdom finally came at the end of a week in which she experienced a series of miscommunications from her teachers.

As we discussed her frustrations, I promised to talk with the school to see if there was a way to open the lines of communication so it didn't happen again. That's when it occurred to me that God had just provided a door for me to walk through— a perfect opening to discuss my daughter's own problems with communication.

"Honey," I said, "you know how frustrating it was for you when your teachers didn't tell you what you needed to know? I feel frustrated when I don't know what's going on at school because you don't tell me. I need to know what's happening if I'm going to be able to help you. Do you think you could do better in the future?"

Yes, came the answer—and without any defensiveness.

God has a thousand ways to give us the wisdom we need, but we need to ask for it and wait for it. If we let fear, anger, desire, or busyness push us to act before we have the wisdom to act rightly, we'll miss out on the blessings wisdom can bring.

Friday

PROMISES ASSOCIATED WITH GOD'S WISDOM

If you don't mind sadness, poverty, foolishness, and a short life, don't bother asking for wisdom. You can get along fine without it. But if you'd rather experience joy, riches, honor, life, understanding, and God's protection, pray that he will bless you with all the wisdom you can handle. Pray, too, for those in leadership whose decisions affect many others—that they will act wisely on behalf of all.

In addition to praying for it, you can actively seek wisdom by cultivating a life of humility, study, patience, and openness to the counsel of others. God's wisdom, the Bible says, is a treasure greater than rubies. Though that treasure may look like folly to the world, no human understanding or plan can stand against it.

Promises in Scripture

> These men turn from the right way
>   to walk down dark paths.
> They take pleasure in doing wrong,
>   and they enjoy the twisted ways of evil.
> Their actions are crooked,
>   and their ways are wrong.
>
> Wisdom will save you from the immoral
>   woman,
>   from the seductive words of the
>   promiscuous woman.
> She has abandoned her husband
>   and ignores the covenant she made
>   before God.

Entering her house leads to death;
    it is the road to the grave.

PROVERBS 2:13-18

No human wisdom or understanding or plan
    can stand against the LORD.

PROVERBS 21:30

The message of the cross is foolish to those who are headed for destruction! But we who are being saved know it is the very power of God.

1 CORINTHIANS 1:18

Continued Prayer and Praise

Proverbs 13:10
Isaiah 11:2
Jeremiah 10:12
Daniel 2:20-23
Matthew 13:54
Luke 2:52
Romans 11:33-34
1 Corinthians 1:18-30
Colossians 2:6-23
James 1:5
James 3:13-17

GOD HAS NO LIMITS

ETERNAL, SELF-SUFFICIENT

His Nature

God is the only being in the universe who is entirely independent, needing nothing and no one to sustain him. Unfettered by time, he exists in eternity. Able to see past, present, and future at once, he is never surprised or taken off guard by anything that has ever happened or will happen. Though his eternal, self-sufficient nature may make him seem remote, these qualities offer us reasons for hope and courage because we are connected to a God who not only exists eternally but also loves eternally. Out of his own self-sufficiency, he can nourish and sustain us.

Key Scripture

> The eternal God is your refuge,
> and his everlasting arms are under you.
> DEUTERONOMY 33:27

Monday

GOD REVEALS HIMSELF

There is no one like the God of Israel.
    He rides across the heavens to help you,
    across the skies in majestic splendor.
The eternal God is your refuge,
    and his everlasting arms are under you.
He drives out the enemy before you;
    he cries out, "Destroy them!"

DEUTERONOMY 33:26-27

Have you never heard?
    Have you never understood?
The LORD is the everlasting God,
    the Creator of all the earth.
He never grows weak or weary.
    No one can measure the depths
        of his understanding.
He gives power to the weak
    and strength to the powerless.
Even youths will become weak
        and tired,
    and young men will fall in exhaustion.
But those who trust in the LORD will
        find new strength.
    They will soar high on wings like
        eagles.
They will run and not grow weary.
    They will walk and not faint.

ISAIAH 40:28-31

Understanding His Eternal Nature

To say that God is eternal is to say that he exists apart from time. Though God is present in our world, he is not confined in time as we are. Existing in eternity, he sees everything that has ever happened, is happening, and will happen. God never has to wait for anything; he never has to wonder what will happen. He can't grow and he doesn't have potential, because he is already everything he will ever be. Existing in perfect completeness before the world began, he will continue to exist in perfect completeness when the world ends.

One of God's titles in the Hebrew Scriptures is *El Olam*, which can be translated "everlasting God" or "eternal God." The word *'ôlām* occurs more than four hundred times in the Old Testament. Translated as "eternal," "everlasting," "forever," "lasting," "ever," "ancient," the word is applied to God and to his Word, laws, covenant, name, reign, love, salvation, and light.

As creatures, we are dependent. We cannot survive unless someone outside ourselves nourishes and sustains us. But God needs no one and nothing. Living in eternity, he is self-sufficient. But he is also the one who sustains us, giving us everything we need to survive—food, water, air to breathe.

Though human beings are mortal, God has placed eternity in our hearts (Ecclesiastes 3:11), designing us to live with him forever. Through Christ's suffering, death, and resurrection, death's power is defeated, and we are redeemed—eternally redeemed.

Lord, you are the everlasting King, the one who is, who was, and who is to come. Thank you for all the ways you have already provided for me, promising to love and care for me forever. There is no one like you. You alone are the everlasting God, the Creator of all the earth! May your Kingdom and your reign and your power be established forever and ever. Amen.

Studying His Eternal Nature and Self-Sufficiency

1. Is it logically necessary for God to be eternal? Why or why not?

2. What does Scripture mean when it says that "his everlasting arms are under you"? Have you ever experienced God in this way? If so, how?

3. Note that Isaiah speaks of the "everlasting God" and then quickly identifies him as the Creator. Why do you think it's easier for us to place our trust in creatures rather than the Creator?

4. What do you need, in this moment, from God? Ask him for it, and then tell him you want to learn to depend on him.

Tuesday

PRAYING IN LIGHT OF GOD'S ETERNAL NATURE

Give thanks to the God of heaven.
His faithful love endures forever.

PSALM 136:26

God has made everything beautiful for its own time. He has planted eternity in the human heart, but even so, people cannot see the whole scope of God's work from beginning to end.

ECCLESIASTES 3:11

Reflect On:	Psalm 136:26; Ecclesiastes 3:11
Praise God:	For his eternal love
Offer Thanks:	That God is not limited by time
Confess:	Your inability to understand the scope of God's work
Ask God:	To help you live every day with an eternal perspective

The idea of eternity is difficult to grasp, like trying to toss a lasso around Mount Everest or cup the Milky Way in your hands. I remember thinking about it as a young child. For some reason I was fascinated by the idea of hell being eternal. Every time I got close to understanding that word *eternity*, particularly in connection with hell, I felt overwhelmed, like I was about to pitch off the edge of a cliff. I'm not sure why I fixated on hell rather than heaven. Perhaps it was for the same reason some children like to watch scary movies or ride roller coasters—it was thrilling.

But what does it mean to say that God is eternal? It means he exists beyond time. He is without beginning or end. Time is part of the world he created, but he is not contained in time. In a way we cannot fathom, God is able to perceive the past, the present, and the future in an everlasting now. All events are present to him. He is never kept in suspense and never has to wonder or worry, because he already knows everything that has happened, is happening, or will happen. For him there is no yesterday and no tomorrow, as all times are equally present to him.

A. W. Tozer, citing C. S. Lewis, explains, "If you could think of a sheet of paper infinitely extended in all directions, and if you took a pencil and made a line one inch long on it, that would be time. When you started to push your pencil it was the beginning of time and when you lifted it off the paper it was the end of time. And all around, infinitely extended in all directions, is God."[1]

But what difference does God's eternal nature make to human beings whose lives in time are immeasurably small? We're like the grass that withers and the flowers that fade. Isn't it depressing to realize how short life is? In one sense, yes. But coming to terms with the brevity of life can lead us to wonder why an infinite, eternal God would even bother to care about us. Why go to any trouble for mere specks on a tiny time line? Why make the ultimate investment—sacrificing his Son for our sakes?

The answer comes from Scripture itself. Though we live in time, God created us for eternity. God loved us so much that he embedded a critical design feature in our nature: he placed eternity in our hearts. How else could we know that his love endures forever unless we have eternity to experience that love?

Wednesday

PRAYING IN LIGHT OF
GOD'S ETERNAL NATURE

In your great mercy you did not abandon them to die in the wilderness. The pillar of cloud still led them forward by day, and the pillar of fire showed them the way through the night. You sent your good Spirit to instruct them, and you did not stop giving them manna from heaven or water for their thirst. For forty years you sustained them in the wilderness, and they lacked nothing. Their clothes did not wear out, and their feet did not swell!

NEHEMIAH 9:19-21

If I were hungry, I would not tell you,
for all the world is mine and everything in it.

PSALM 50:12

The eyes of all look to you in hope;
you give them their food as they need it.
When you open your hand,
you satisfy the hunger and thirst of every
living thing.

PSALM 145:15-16

Reflect On:	Nehemiah 9:19-21; Psalm 50:12; 145:15-16
Praise God:	For making everything from nothing
Offer Thanks:	For the way God has sustained you from the moment of your conception until now
Confess:	Any lack of gratitude for God's provision
Ask God:	To sustain you with his grace and strength so you can do his will

"In a hole in the ground there lived a hobbit. Not a nasty, dirty, wet hole, filled with the ends of worms and an oozy smell, nor yet a dry, bare, sandy hole with nothing in it to sit down on or to eat: it was a hobbit-hole, and that means comfort."[2] So begins J. R. R. Tolkien's classic tale *The Hobbit*.

Last week I thought I caught a glimpse of one of those hobbit-holes, a place Bilbo Baggins himself might fancy living in. But the home, it turns out, is not in the Shire; it's in New Mexico. Featured on a television show about extreme homes, this one is called an Earthship because it's designed to function off the grid, with no need to connect to electricity, gas, or water. Though the shape of the house is organic and rather bizarre, the idea of owning a self-sustaining home with zero utility bills is appealing.

Constructed primarily of found materials, its heavy walls are made of steel-belted automobile tires crammed with dirt and then staggered and stacked like bricks. Since scrap tires are everywhere, it's a cheap and sustainable resource.

Need water for drinking, showering, laundering? The house harvests water from rain, condensation, and snow, recycling it in order to flush toilets and water plants. Need heat or cooling? A comfortable interior climate is maintained with the help of large front windows with shades, and heat that's absorbed in the load-bearing walls. Need to power up your cell phone or computer? Electricity is provided through wind turbines and photovoltaic panels that convert solar energy.

Pretty neat if you can satisfy the local building codes and you don't mind having the most unusual home on the block. But even an Earthship like this won't really make you self-sufficient. You still need things like food, water, medical care, and human companionship to sustain yourself. By contrast, God needs nothing but himself to continue to exist.

To survive on this planet, we have to depend on everything God made. Every proton, every electron, every neutron is part of God's creative work. If he were to withdraw for even a moment, the universe would simply collapse, and every living thing would cease to be. But thanks be to God, because he lovingly upholds the world he has made. Today let's praise him—not only for making us, but for giving us what we need to sustain our lives.

Thursday

PRAYING IN LIGHT OF GOD'S ETERNAL NATURE

Trust in the LORD always,
for the LORD GOD is the eternal Rock.

ISAIAH 26:4

You must not forget this one thing, dear friends: A day is like a thousand years to the Lord, and a thousand years is like a day.

2 PETER 3:8

Reflect On: Isaiah 26:4; 2 Peter 3:8
Praise God: Because he dwells in eternity
Offer Thanks: That the Lord has your eternal interests in view
Confess: Any tendency to open your life to anxiety because you don't want to admit your limitations
Ask God: To help you order your life in a way that minimizes needless worry

I remember driving across Montana with a friend when I was in my early twenties. We loved the signs on the highway that instructed us to drive at a "reasonable and prudent" speed. To us that meant there was no speed limit. We could go as fast as our little hearts desired. So we did, crossing Montana in record time.

Unlike twentysomethings, God has no limits, because he doesn't need them. In fact, the reverse is true. To state it rather

173

awkwardly, God *needs* to have no limits, or else he wouldn't be God. If he were partially wise, for instance, he would make mistakes. If he were somewhat powerful, he would at times be weak. If he were usually trustworthy, he would not always be faithful. Similarly, God is unlimited when it comes to time. Perhaps that's why he never gets panicky, rushed, or frantic.

Not long ago I had several errands to complete, the last of which was to get to the pharmacy before it closed. With no time to spare, I dropped off my daughter at her karate class, drove to my mother's for a brief visit, picked my daughter up after her class, stopped at a fast-food restaurant for sandwiches and chips, and then dropped my daughter off at home. Just as I was backing out of the driveway on my way to the pharmacy, she came running out of the house, waving her hands. Knowing I had only a couple of minutes to spare, I felt a knot of anxiety forming in my throat, then moving into my face and pinching it into a complaint as I rolled down the window to find out what was wrong. Luci had simply forgotten to take the chips out of the car, and dinner couldn't be enjoyed without them. I left in a huff, irritated at the thought that I might be late to the pharmacy.

That tense little encounter with my daughter almost made me laugh except that it was so ridiculously sad. Yes, it was good to deliver my daughter to her class, visit my mother, make sure my daughter got fed, and pick up the medicine we needed, but scheduling everything so tightly had sent me into a panic. I was making a big problem out of a little one.

Fortunately, the eternal God never loses perspective, never gets anxious, never feels pressured. He sees the end from the beginning, rather than sequentially in time.

Asking for prayers for her gravely ill husband, Anne Graham Lotz cited a prayer her mother had written in the flyleaf of Anne's Bible years earlier:

Trusting Him when dark doubts assail us
Trusting Him when our strength is small
Trusting Him when to simply trust Him
is the hardest thing of all.[3]

That is our task too. To simply trust God.

Join me today in praying that the Lord will ease our hearts, helping us to trust him for all the small and large moments in our lives. Let's ask for the grace to remember that we needn't be consumed by anxiety, because we belong to a God who, knowing everything, worries about nothing.

Friday

PROMISES ASSOCIATED WITH GOD'S ETERNAL NATURE

God has promised us many things. One of the greatest of these is heaven. Holding on to this promise is like placing your hand around a sturdy climbing hold embedded in the face of a cliff. Knowing that heaven is part of your future will help you scale life's challenges with more confidence.

But many of us are so preoccupied with tomorrow and the day after that we rarely think of spending eternity with God. C. S. Lewis highlights this mistake in *The Screwtape Letters*. Here's how a senior devil advises a junior devil in demonic strategy: "We want a whole race perpetually in pursuit of the rainbow's end, never honest, nor kind, nor happy *now*."[4] Rather than investing in the present in a way that will prepare us for heaven, we expend our energy on an earthly future that we cannot see and that likely won't exist—at least not in the way we think it will.

But God wants us to realize that we are citizens of a Kingdom that will last forever. Listen to what Psalm 100 says: "The Lord is good. His unfailing love continues forever" (v. 5). Why would the psalmist say God's love endures forever if there were no one for him to love forever? And why would Paul tell Titus that God promised eternal life "before the world began" (1:2) unless God's promise is rooted in eternity itself?

Let's stop thinking of heaven as some vague place up in the clouds and start thinking of it as a biblical reality toward which our lives are aimed. Let's thank God, too, that we've been born again—not to a life that will quickly end, but to one that will last forever.

Promises in Scripture

> Enter his gates with thanksgiving;
>> go into his courts with praise.
>> Give thanks to him and praise his name.
> For the LORD is good.
>> His unfailing love continues forever,
>> and his faithfulness continues to each
>>> generation.

PSALM 100:4-5

My sheep listen to my voice; I know them, and they follow me. I give them eternal life, and they will never perish. No one can snatch them away from me, for my Father has given them to me, and he is more powerful than anyone else. No one can snatch them from the Father's hand.

JOHN 10:27-29

I [Paul] have been sent to proclaim faith to those God has chosen and to teach them to know the truth that shows them how to live godly lives. This truth gives them confidence that they have eternal life, which God—who does not lie—promised them before the world began.

TITUS 1:1-2

You have been born again, but not to a life that will quickly end. Your new life will last forever because it comes from the eternal, living word of God.

1 PETER 1:23

Continued Prayer and Praise

Genesis 9:16
1 Chronicles 17:27
Psalm 119:89, 142
Matthew 18:8-9

Matthew 19:29
John 1:1-2
John 5:24
John 17:3
Acts 17:25
Romans 1:20
2 Corinthians 5:1
2 Thessalonians 1:7-10
1 Peter 5:10

GOD IS
A LOVER

JEALOUS

His Nature

Most of us think of jealousy as a negative trait. Described as the "green-eyed monster," it can poison relationships. When applied to God, it conjures a frightening picture. How can an all-good God be described as jealous? Why does the Bible repeatedly portray him as a jealous husband who will not tolerate unfaithfulness? To conclude that jealousy is beneath God would be to miss the nature of his holiness and the passionate quality of his love for us.

Though the Bible doesn't provide a definition of divine jealousy, neither does it portray jealousy as something that diminishes God in any way. If anything, Scripture emphasizes his right to protect and pursue the people he loves as well as his right to protect his honor. Even the New Testament emphasizes the exclusivity of God's claim on our lives. Jesus said, "I am the way, the truth, and the life. No one can come to the Father except through me" (John 14:6).

Unlike human jealousy, which often springs from self-love, divine jealousy is a reflection of God's holiness and of his passionate love and faithfulness.

Key Scripture

You must worship no other gods, for the LORD, whose very name is Jealous, is a God who is jealous about his relationship with you.

EXODUS 34:14

Monday

GOD REVEALS HIMSELF

Be very careful never to make a treaty with the people who live in the land where you are going. If you do, you will follow their evil ways and be trapped. Instead, you must break down their pagan altars, smash their sacred pillars, and cut down their Asherah poles. You must worship no other gods, for the LORD, whose very name is Jealous, is a God who is jealous about his relationship with you.

You must not make a treaty of any kind with the people living in the land. They lust after their gods, offering sacrifices to them. They will invite you to join them in their sacrificial meals, and you will go with them. Then you will accept their daughters, who sacrifice to other gods, as wives for your sons. And they will seduce your sons to commit adultery against me by worshiping other gods. You must not make any gods of molten metal for yourselves.

EXODUS 34:12-17

Understanding His Jealousy
The Bible contains descriptions of God that can be disturbing. Perhaps the most difficult portrayals for us to accept are those that have to do with God's wrath and jealousy. How can we fully trust ourselves to a divine being who displays such characteristics?

Part of our difficulty stems from the fact that we want God to fit a certain mold. For many of us, the ideal god is nice, kind, powerful, affectionate, and safe. He's someone we can easily understand, someone who doesn't demand too much. But is such a god up to the task of being God? Can we trust our lives to him? Is he great enough to worship?

The God of the Bible is ultimately mysterious—altogether

different from us—though we share his likeness in certain respects. As such, it makes sense that we approach him with healthy fear, not daring to sit in judgment on his character.

The second problem is that we sometimes fail to understand that the Bible's description of God as jealous is an anthropomorphism. God speaks to us using limited human words that can't adequately describe him. God's anger and jealousy differ from ours because, unlike us, God always acts in a way that reflects his goodness and justice.

In Hebrew the noun *qin'â* can be translated "jealousy," "zeal," "jealous anger," "envy," or "jealous."

The Greek noun *zēlos* is used in the New Testament and can be translated "jealousy," "envy," "zeal," "passion," "ardent concern," or "enthusiasm."

In both the Old and the New Testaments, jealousy is often portrayed in negative terms. Human jealousy is dangerous and damaging, as evidenced in the stories of Joseph and his brothers and Saul and David.

But God is rightly jealous for his honor, his glory, and his name. His jealousy extends to his people and is manifested by his watchful care, lest they be led astray.

It's interesting to note that the Hebrew and Greek words for jealousy are the same words that are used for zeal or zealous. Though human beings can become overzealous, Scripture affirms godly zeal, which is a rightful concern for God's honor and interests.

Lord, I want to be jealous for your honor and glory. Help me to express that jealousy by guarding my mind and my heart so they do not stray from you. I want to worship you alone.

Studying His Jealousy

1. What images of God come to mind when you think of jealousy? How do they make you feel?
2. In the passage from Exodus, God warns his people against allying themselves with foreigners. What reason does he give for this?
3. What does God's jealousy reveal about him?
4. How should we think about God's jealousy in our own lives?
5. Have you ever observed a person who showed zeal for God? If so, describe him or her.

Tuesday

PRAYING IN LIGHT OF GOD'S JEALOUSY

You must not have any other god but me.

You must not make for yourself an idol of any kind or an image of anything in the heavens or on the earth or in the sea. You must not bow down to them or worship them, for I, the LORD your God, am a jealous God who will not tolerate your affection for any other gods. I lay the sins of the parents upon their children; the entire family is affected—even children in the third and fourth generations of those who reject me.

EXODUS 20:3-5

[Jesus'] disciples remembered that it was written, "Zeal for your house will consume me."

JOHN 2:17, ESV

Reflect On: Exodus 20:3-5; John 2:17
Praise God: Because he alone is worthy of our worship
Offer Thanks: For God's great love
Confess: Any indifference to the plight of those who do
               not yet know God
Ask God: To fill you with a holy zeal

I remember how shocked I was when I toured a Buddhist temple during a trip to China. It wasn't the great, golden idols with their stylized grimaces that set me off. Nor was it the sticks of burning incense, symbolizing prayers that were being offered. At the time these seemed like fascinating artifacts of an unfamiliar culture. As we left the temple, a friend mentioned how troubled she was by the scene. It struck me that while she had felt distressed at the sight of hundreds of people praying to idols, I had been playing the role of detached observer, approaching the experience as an interesting cultural event. My lack of concern for souls who were lost, without Christ, shocked me. How could my heart, I wondered, be so far from the heart of God?

Scripture speaks not of a tepid or an indifferent god but of a divine being whose love is all consuming. While we can accept the idea of God as a passionate lover, we recoil from the notion that he is also a jealous lover. Divine jealousy sounds terrifying—not to mention far beneath the dignity of a God of love. But is it?

We know, of course, that jealousy can devastate human relationships. We also know that our jealous feelings usually stem from insecurity and self-centeredness. Not wanting to ascribe such characteristics to God, we often ignore or try to explain away Scriptures that speak of his jealousy. Part of our difficulty stems from the fact that we don't understand how jealousy works in God compared with how it works in humans.

People become jealous when they perceive a threat to their exclusive claim on another person. They want that person to be theirs and theirs alone. In the world of human relationships, jealousy can sometimes preserve monogamous relationships. But jealousy can also destroy relationships when it becomes a desire for possession and control. To quote one writer, "Jealousy is the desire to be god to another."[1]

God's jealousy is far different from human jealousy because it is based on two realities. The first is that God has a right to us. He created us, and we belong to him. Second, he knows that human beings can be happy only to the degree that we are united with him. If we pay homage to false gods (in our culture, that may be money, drugs, sex, power, or relationships), we are spurning his love, acting the part of an unfaithful spouse. Because God knows that giving ourselves to anything less than him will result in our ruin, jealousy is the proper response.

I like the way the British preacher George Morrison explains it: "Only God can satisfy the heart," he says, "even the poorest and the meanest heart. Only He can absorb it without wronging it, for in Him we live and move and have our being. . . . But the jealousy of man grows dark and terrible because it makes a claim that is impossible. But for God, the jealousy is His right."[2]

How should we respond to God's jealousy? By forsaking whatever separates us from him and by reflecting his passionate concern for others. We must become zealous for his honor, his glory and his gospel, recognizing how desperately the world needs to know him. Join me today in praying for the grace to heed Paul's call to the Romans that they would never be lacking in zeal (Romans 12:11, NIV).

Wednesday

PRAYING IN LIGHT OF GOD'S JEALOUSY

You must worship no other gods, for the LORD, whose very name is Jealous, is a God who is jealous about his relationship with you.

EXODUS 34:14

If you love your father or mother more than you love me, you are not worthy of being mine; or if you love your son or daughter more than me, you are not worthy of being mine. If you refuse to take up your cross and follow me, you are not worthy of being mine. If you cling to your life, you will lose it; but if you give up your life for me, you will find it.

MATTHEW 10:37-39

Reflect On: Exodus 34:14; Matthew 10:37-39
Praise God: For being worthy of your total devotion
Offer Thanks: Because his jealousy produces a protective attitude toward you
Confess: Any tendency to put other relationships before your relationship with God
Ask God: To watch over you

Amy Winehouse was one of the world's most acclaimed singers, known for her eclectic mix of jazz, pop, soul, and R & B. In 2008 she reprised a song recorded by more than fifty other performers, including such greats as Frank Sinatra, Willie Nelson, Etta James, Roberta Flack, and Barbra Streisand. Written by George and Ira Gershwin in 1926, the song "Someone to Watch over Me" expresses the universal longing for that one special person

189

who will always be there for us, who will always have our best interests at heart.

Maybe you know the lyrics, which speak of a little lamb being lost in the woods but that would learn to be good to someone who would watch over it.

Three years after recording the song, Amy Winehouse was gone, having never found the love and protection she sang about. At the age of twenty-seven, after years of drug and alcohol abuse, she died as a result of alcohol poisoning.

Why bring up another sad story of a great talent self-destructing? Simply to point out that in the end, God is the only one who can satisfy the yearnings of a thousand love songs. Only his passionate love and his watchful care are strong enough to straighten us out and set us on the right track.

Indeed, God is jealous when it comes to loving us. He won't settle for half of our hearts. With him, it's everything or nothing.

As we reflect on a story so tragic and a love so great, let us turn to God, admitting that we're not so different from the little lamb Amy Winehouse sang about—the one that was lost in the woods but knew it would be good to the one who watched over it.

Thursday

PRAYING IN LIGHT OF GOD'S JEALOUSY

This is how God loved the world: He gave his one and only Son, so that everyone who believes in him will not perish but have eternal life. God sent his Son into the world not to judge the world, but to save the world through him.

JOHN 3:16-17

Reflect On:	John 3:16-17
Praise God:	For loving us despite our sins
Offer Thanks:	That God will not let us go
Confess:	Any resistance to God's exclusive claims on you
Ask God:	To help you be faithful to your relationship with him

Imagine that your marriage is facing a crisis. Your husband or wife has just learned a secret you have been trying to keep— that you are having an affair. But as you discuss the matter with your spouse, your fears about a confrontation evaporate because the person you're married to seems completely indifferent to the news of your betrayal. You realize there will be no big emotional explosion. There is no crisis. Instead of expressing anger or jealousy, your partner simply says that you are an adult who is free to do as you please. You can stay home whenever you like or go out with someone else. It really doesn't matter.

What would you think? Would you grieve because you realize that you've cheated on someone who would have done anything for you, even laying down his or her life if necessary? Would you be sad, knowing you are turning your back on one of the world's great marriages? I hardly think so. If you grieved at all, your hurt would come from knowing your spouse cared little for you.

Fortunately, God is the opposite of an indifferent husband. In one of the most poignant stories of the Bible, he tells the prophet Hosea to marry a prostitute named Gomer. Hosea's life will be full of pain and heartbreak, a lived-out parable that exposes God's broken heart. God has wed himself to faithless Israel, who has repeatedly betrayed him. Refusing to give up on his beloved people, he tells Hosea, "Go and love your wife again, even though she commits adultery with another lover. This will illustrate that the LORD still loves Israel, even though the people have turned to other gods and love to worship them" (Hosea 3:1).

We needn't provoke God to jealousy in order to probe the depths of his love. Instead, let's celebrate our relationship with him and be grateful we have a God who will do anything for us, even laying down his life, so we can be reconciled to him.

Friday

PROMISES ASSOCIATED WITH GOD'S JEALOUSY

The woman in the Song of Songs knows the enduring power of love. She speaks of a love so deep and strong it can withstand elemental threats like death and floods. It is strong and "flashes like fire, the brightest kind of flame" (8:6). Her passionate response to the man she loves images what our own response to God can be. Like her, we can ask God to place us as a seal over his heart—a seal that will never be broken because of the intensity of his love, which is as strong as death, its jealousy as enduring as the grave.

Promises in Scripture

> Place me like a seal over your heart,
>   like a seal on your arm.
> For love is as strong as death,
>   its jealousy as enduring as the grave.
> Love flashes like fire,
>   the brightest kind of flame.

SONG OF SONGS 8:6

This is what the Sovereign LORD says: I will end the captivity of my people; I will have mercy on all Israel, for I jealously guard my holy reputation!

EZEKIEL 39:25

> The LORD will pity his people
>   and jealously guard the honor of his land.

JOEL 2:18

Did God's people stumble and fall beyond recovery? Of course not! They were disobedient, so God made salvation available to the Gentiles. But he wanted his own people to become jealous and claim it for themselves.

ROMANS 11:11

Continued Prayer and Praise

Numbers 25:10-13
Deuteronomy 4:23-40
Joshua 24:15-27
Ezekiel 39:21-29
Zechariah 1:12-17
2 Corinthians 11:2

12

GOD IS
ALWAYS FAIR

Just, Righteous

His Nature

Justice resides within the very nature of God, who always does what is morally right and who commands us to do the same. If God were merciful but not just, he might be a "nice" god or a weak god or something even worse, because for someone to let evil go unpunished when he has the power to do something about it is to become an accessory to evil.

Without justice, community is violated and relationships disintegrate. Though God hates sins against justice, Scripture describes God as being slow to anger, eager to allow as many people as possible to come into his Kingdom through faith in his Son. His judgment is constrained by his mercy.

When we belong to Christ and repent of our sins, we no longer need to fear God's judgment. Instead, his justice becomes a source of hope and joy, because we realize it forms the foundation for peace and harmony—both in our personal lives and in the world around us.

Key Scripture

The King will say to those on his right, "Come, you who are blessed by my Father, inherit the Kingdom prepared for you from the creation of the world. For I was hungry, and you fed me. I was thirsty, and you gave me a drink. I was a stranger, and you invited me into your home. I was naked, and you gave me clothing. I was sick, and you cared for me. I was in prison, and you visited me."

MATTHEW 25:34-36

197

Monday

GOD REVEALS HIMSELF

As the Scriptures say,

> "No one is righteous—
> not even one."
>
> ROMANS 3:10

When the Son of Man comes in his glory, and all the angels with him, then he will sit upon his glorious throne. All the nations will be gathered in his presence, and he will separate the people as a shepherd separates the sheep from the goats. He will place the sheep at his right hand and the goats at his left.

Then the King will say to those on his right, "Come, you who are blessed by my Father, inherit the Kingdom prepared for you from the creation of the world. For I was hungry, and you fed me. I was thirsty, and you gave me a drink. I was a stranger, and you invited me into your home. I was naked, and you gave me clothing. I was sick, and you cared for me. I was in prison, and you visited me."

Then these righteous ones will reply, "Lord, when did we ever see you hungry and feed you? Or thirsty and give you something to drink? Or a stranger and show you hospitality? Or naked and give you clothing? When did we ever see you sick or in prison and visit you?"

And the King will say, "I tell you the truth, when you did it to one of the least of these my brothers and sisters, you were doing it to me!"

> MATTHEW 25:31-40

Understanding His Justice

The primary Hebrew word for justice is *tsedeq*. It is frequently translated "righteousness," "righteous," "honest," or "right."

Righteousness is a biblical word that means being in right relationship with God and, consequently, with others. By contrast, injustice fractures and destroys relationships. As the theology professor Addison Leitch says, righteousness "is primarily and basically a relationship, never an attainment." For the Christian, righteousness "is a direction, a loyalty, a commitment, a hope—and only someday an arrival."[1]

Many people in Western societies think of justice as being performed in a courtroom, where an impartial judgment is rendered according to the laws of society. But this was not the cultural context of the Bible. As Leitch observes, "For the judge in Israel, righteousness is more the fulfillment of the demands of the community for balance and harmony. The judge wishes to restore the righteousness of the community, and in some cases may therefore give one of the parties not his just due, but his overdue. Righteous judgments are protective and restoring."[2] No wonder the Hebrew prophets cried out on behalf of the poor and downtrodden.

God's justice is the foundation for lasting peace and true harmony. Ultimately justice is rooted not in a system of laws or regulations but in who God is—in his nature and character. To be attracted to justice is to be attracted to God.

Though it is impossible to become righteous on our own, Paul tells the Corinthians that Christ has become our righteousness (1 Corinthians 1:30, NIV). He has satisfied the demands of justice by dying for our sins and being raised from the dead. By doing so, he bore the heaviest burden in our struggle against evil, enabling those who believe in him to come into a life-giving relationship with God.

But righteousness cannot be forced. Those who love their sins and refuse to follow Christ will ultimately face judgment. To blame God for this state of affairs is like blaming fire for burning up a piece of paper. Just as fire and paper cannot coexist, neither can justice and sin.

It is only because of Jesus, who is called the "righteous one" (Acts 3:14) and the "righteous Judge" (2 Timothy 4:8), that we have the privilege of entering the presence of God, the "righteous Father" (John 17:25). Through Jesus, we have peace with God and one another.

You are Jehovah-Tsidkenu, the Lord our Righteousness—the one who can neither disregard justice nor discard love. Seeing my sin, you had to condemn it. But you didn't condemn me. Thank you for the gift of your Son and for the atonement he made for sin. Let me praise you daily by seeking justice and by doing what is right in your eyes.

Studying His Justice

1. What comes to mind when you hear the word *righteousness?*
2. What makes self-righteousness so unattractive?
3. What does Jesus imply about the "righteous ones" in the passage from Matthew 25?
4. What emotions does the phrase "final judgment" evoke in you? Why?
5. Do you think Christians are called to engage in social justice? Why or why not?

Tuesday

PRAYING IN LIGHT OF GOD'S JUSTICE

Defend the weak and the fatherless;
uphold the cause of the poor and the oppressed.

PSALM 82:3, NIV

I want to see a mighty flood of justice,
an endless river of righteous living.

AMOS 5:24

God blesses those who hunger and thirst for justice,
for they will be satisfied.

MATTHEW 5:6

Reflect On: Psalm 82:3; Amos 5:24; Matthew 5:6
Praise God: For caring about the weak and the fatherless
Offer Thanks: For the call to reflect God's heart to the poor
and oppressed
Confess: Any indifference toward those who suffer from
injustice
Ask God: To help you defend the weak

I can remember only a few times when I was a victim of injustice. Each time, someone had tried to cheat me out of something that belonged to me. I felt so angry that I wanted to fight back with all the power I could muster. And I did.

But what about people who suffer from injustice on a daily basis? Perhaps they have had the bad luck of being born into poverty or maybe they are members of a racial minority or perhaps they have a disability or a mental illness that makes them easy targets for con artists. And what about those who can't fight back for themselves? They may be children who are terrorized by the adults who should be protecting them. These children's lives may be one long struggle against evils they don't have the power to overcome. What does justice look like for them?

I know I should care more about those people than I do about my privileged self, but I don't—at least not yet. I want to be more like Bob Pierce, the man who founded World Vision and Samaritan's Purse. Years ago, after visiting suffering children in Korea, he wrote this prayer on the flyleaf of his Bible: "Let my heart be broken with the things that break the heart of God."

According to writer Tim Stafford, when Franklin Graham asked Pierce how to "shake people out of their complacency," Pierce replied that he had "become a part of the suffering. I literally felt the child's blindness, the mother's grief. . . . It was all too real to me when I stood before an audience." Pastor Richard Halvorsen says that Pierce "prayed more earnestly and importunely than anyone else I have ever known. It was as though prayer burned within him. . . . Bob Pierce functioned from a broken heart."[3]

Though Pierce had his share of personal challenges, it seems to me he lived out the beatitude that says, "Blessed are those who hunger and thirst for righteousness, for they will be filled" (Matthew 5:6, NIV). Perhaps you and I need to become more like Bob Pierce, letting God break our hearts with the things that break his.

Wednesday

PRAYING IN LIGHT OF GOD'S JUSTICE

Jesus said, "There was a certain rich man who was splendidly clothed in purple and fine linen and who lived each day in luxury. At his gate lay a poor man named Lazarus who was covered with sores. As Lazarus lay there longing for scraps from the rich man's table, the dogs would come and lick his open sores.

"Finally, the poor man died and was carried by the angels to be with Abraham. The rich man also died and was buried, and his soul went to the place of the dead. There, in torment, he saw Abraham in the far distance with Lazarus at his side.

"The rich man shouted, 'Father Abraham, have some pity! Send Lazarus over here to dip the tip of his finger in water and cool my tongue. I am in anguish in these flames.'

"But Abraham said to him, 'Son, remember that during your life-time you had everything you wanted, and Lazarus had nothing. So now he is here being comforted, and you are in anguish.'"

LUKE 16:19-25

Reflect On: Luke 16:19-25
Praise God: Because his justice will prevail
Offer Thanks: For the chance to serve the poor
Confess: Any selfishness or fear that keeps you from being
                generous to others
Ask God: To help you hunger and thirst for justice

A few years ago someone published a Bible study that revolved around an unusual theme: the morality of James Bond. The study, which bears the title *Ian Fleming's Seven Deadlier Sins and*

007's Moral Compass, focuses on the theme of the seven deadly sins as it threads its way through Ian Fleming's novels. The publisher calls it "a book that will usefully disturb you."

I wonder how often I am "usefully disturbed" by the things that disturb God. Have I become dull to certain kinds of sins, afraid to speak against injustice lest others dislike me? I'm not thinking about obvious sins like robbery or rape but about the sins our culture cherishes—those linked to pleasure and convenience. How tolerant am I, for instance, of greed, gluttony, and sexual immorality?

In the midst of a down economy, it has become easier to see the devastation avarice can inflict on innocent people, many of whom have become impoverished because of the greed of others. Sadly, many of us have turned a blind eye to greed because we've so heartily embraced the values of a materialistic culture. Where, I wonder, is greed operating in my own life?

What about gluttony—a sin rarely on my radar? How can I take care of the body God has given me, resisting the lure of a culture that celebrates gluttony? What is the church doing to warn against its dangers and to help those ensnared by it?

And what about sexual immorality? Hasn't the lack of restraint in sexual behavior forced many more women and children into poverty by contributing to the decline of family life? How can I join with others to help people see the beauty of committing themselves to one person for life? How can I let people know that they have much to lose when it comes to engaging in premarital or extramarital sex?

When Jesus said, "You will always have the poor among you" (Matthew 26:11), surely he wasn't telling us to disregard them. How is he calling me to help? How can I remember to focus not merely on the poor that I can see but on the poor I cannot see, including unborn children?

When it comes to justice, the prophet Micah poses a critical question: "What does the LORD require of you?" And then comes his eloquent answer: "To act justly and to love mercy and to walk humbly with your God" (Micah 6:8, NIV). This is our calling as Christians: to reflect the heart of the God we love.

Thursday

PRAYING IN LIGHT OF GOD'S JUSTICE

We are all infected and impure with sin.
When we display our righteous deeds,
they are nothing but filthy rags.
Like autumn leaves, we wither and fall,
and our sins sweep us away like
the wind.

ISAIAH 64:6

This is how God loved the world: He gave his one and only Son, so that everyone who believes in him will not perish but have eternal life. God sent his Son into the world not to judge the world, but to save the world through him.

There is no judgment against anyone who believes in him. But anyone who does not believe in him has already been judged for not believing in God's one and only Son. And the judgment is based on this fact: God's light came into the world, but people loved the darkness more than the light, for their actions were evil. . . .

Anyone who believes in God's Son has eternal life. Anyone who doesn't obey the Son will never experience eternal life but remains under God's angry judgment.

JOHN 3:16-19, 36

Reflect On: Isaiah 64:6; John 3:16-19, 36
Praise God: For sending us a Savior
Offer Thanks: For the gift of faith
Confess: Any reluctance to share the gospel with those who don't know Christ
Ask God: To give you a spirit of boldness and love

In 1741 Jonathan Edwards preached one of the most famous sermons in American history. It was later published under the title "Sinners in the Hands of an Angry God." In it Edwards warned about the horrors of hell with such forceful imagery that many people in his listening audience moaned and cried out in repentance.

In the twenty-first century, talk of hell has receded. Some of us doubt there is such a place. We can't fathom the idea that a good God would allow people to go there. But Jesus speaks openly about hell, pointing to a time of judgment in which the unrighteous "will go away into eternal punishment, but the righteous will go into eternal life" (Matthew 25:46).

While none of us need a steady diet of preaching that's focused on hellfire and damnation, it's good to think about hell once in a while, lest we lull ourselves into believing that there's no such place and that nobody we know is headed there. Perhaps we could study what the Bible says or read an old-fashioned sermon on the topic. Developing a biblical view of that worst of all places is like eating our "spiritual spinach"—unappetizing but good for us.

Let me get you started with an adaptation of a sermon delivered by the nineteenth-century pastor Charles Spurgeon, known as the Prince of Preachers. As you tune in, imagine yourself in the audience, watching as Spurgeon strides across the platform, alternating between two voices: one warning of imminent danger and the other trying to soothe and lull you into a false sense of security.

Your hour-glass is emptying every day. All of you, young and old, are standing on a narrow neck of land between two boundless seas—that isthmus of life—narrowing every moment, and you, and you, and you are yet unpardoned.

There is a city to be destroyed and you are in it—soldiers stand at the outskirts with orders to execute anyone who doesn't know the password.

"*Sleep on, sleep on; the attack is not today; sleep on, sleep on. The soldiers are not yet at your door. Sleep on, sleep on.*"

"But the attack will come tomorrow."

"*Yes, sleep on, sleep on; it is not till tomorrow. Sleep on, procrastinate, procrastinate.*"

"Listen! I hear a rumbling noise at the city's outskirts. They're coming."

"*Sleep on, sleep on; the soldiers are not yet at your door. Don't ask for mercy yet. Sleep on, sleep on.*"

"But listen. I hear the screams of men and women. They're dying. They fall, they fall, they fall. Now the soldiers are marching up the stairs."

"*No, sleep on, sleep on; they haven't reached your room yet.*"

"But they just broke down the door!"

"*No, sleep on, sleep on. The knife is not yet at your throat. Sleep on, sleep on!*"

It is at your throat. You wake with terror. Sleep on, sleep on! But you are gone![4]

Spurgeon goes on to address his listeners: "You understand the parable. You don't need me to tell you that death is after you, that justice will eventually be done, that Christ crucified is the only password that can save you. I need not explain how Satan lulls you into thinking you are safe and how knowing God is slow to anger, you are slow to repent."[5]

Spurgeon finishes his sobering sermon by praying that some among his listeners would heed the warning and turn to Christ.

Let's take a moment now to ask God to use us to reach friends and family who are yet far from him. Let's pray for the courage to share the gospel with them so that they might live with Christ forever.

Friday

PROMISES ASSOCIATED WITH GOD'S JUSTICE

Make no mistake: no matter how much evil and unfairness exist on earth, the Lord will eventually give justice to the oppressed. He will lift up the needy and right the wrongs that have been done to those who have been mistreated, punishing those who care nothing for justice. But before the end of the world, when perfect justice will be rendered to all, we have the chance to be used by God to begin fulfilling this promise. Let's do what God is calling us to do. And let's rejoice every time we see a poor person lifted out of poverty, an immigrant succeeding, or a single mother getting the help she needs, because these are intimations of what is to come.

Promises in Scripture

> The LORD gives righteousness
> and justice to all who are treated unfairly.
>
> PSALM 103:6

> He gives justice to the oppressed
> and food to the hungry.
> The LORD frees the prisoners.
> The LORD opens the eyes of the blind.
> The LORD lifts up those who are weighed
> down.
> The LORD loves the godly.
> The LORD protects the foreigners among us.
> He cares for the orphans and widows,
> but he frustrates the plans of the wicked.
>
> PSALM 146:7-9

211

The righteous will shine like the sun in their Father's Kingdom.

MATTHEW 13:43

The earnest prayer of a righteous person has great power and produces wonderful results.

JAMES 5:16

Continued Prayer and Praise
Psalm 15
Psalm 72:1-14
Psalm 98
Isaiah 11:1-5
Isaiah 61
Jeremiah 23:5-6
Luke 5:31-32
Romans 5:12-19
Galatians 2:16

GOD LEANS TOWARD COMPASSION

MERCIFUL

His Nature

One way to gauge the strength of your relationship with God is to examine your thoughts about him. In your heart of hearts, do you see him as quick tempered and easily displeased or as a Father who is kind and merciful? Do you come to him daily, trusting in his kindness, or do you hold back just a little, fearing his rejection?

Scripture assures us that God's anger passes quickly while his mercy endures forever. Like any good father, God is capable of righteous anger when he sees his children hurting themselves or others. But when you belong to his family through faith in Christ, his anger is like one of those brief thunderstorms that pop up in the midst of a long, sunny summer.

When we stumble, God sees not only the stain of our sin but also the misery it leaves behind. Our suffering evokes his mercy. And his mercy is designed to draw us back to him.

Key Scripture

> Yahweh! The LORD!
> The God of compassion and mercy!

EXODUS 34:6

Monday

GOD REVEALS HIMSELF

The LORD came down in a cloud and stood there with him; and he called out his own name, Yahweh. The LORD passed in front of Moses, calling out,

> "Yahweh! The LORD!
>   The God of compassion and mercy!
> I am slow to anger
>   and filled with unfailing love and faithfulness.
> I lavish unfailing love to a thousand generations.
>   I forgive iniquity, rebellion, and sin.
> But I do not excuse the guilty.
>   I lay the sins of the parents upon their children
>   and grandchildren;
> the entire family is affected—
>   even children in the third and fourth
>   generations."

ExODUS 34:5-7

> The LORD is compassionate and merciful,
>   slow to get angry and filled with unfailing love.
> He will not constantly accuse us,
>   nor remain angry forever.
> He does not punish us for all our sins;
>   he does not deal harshly with us, as we deserve.
> For his unfailing love toward those who fear him
>   is as great as the height of the heavens above
>   the earth.
> He has removed our sins as far from us
>   as the east is from the west.

217

The LORD is like a father to his children,
    tender and compassionate to those who
        fear him.
For he knows how weak we are;
    he remembers we are only dust.
Our days on earth are like grass;
    like wildflowers, we bloom and die.
The wind blows, and we are gone—
    as though we had never been here.
But the love of the LORD remains forever
    with those who fear him.
His salvation extends to the children's children
    of those who are faithful to his covenant,
    of those who obey his commandments!

PSALM 103:8-18

Understanding His Mercy

The word *mercy* characterizes God's response to human misery and suffering. It's what moves him to treat us with compassion and kindness even when our suffering is caused by our own sins.

The Hebrew word *hesed* is the word commonly translated "mercy" in the Hebrew Scriptures. Hesed can also be translated as "love," "loving-kindness," "loyalty," "steadfast love," "unfailing love," and "covenant faithfulness." Though human beings can show hesed to one another, hesed often refers to God's covenant relationship with his people.

When Moses asked God to reveal himself, God replied by saying, "I am slow to anger and filled with *hesed* and faithfulness. I lavish *hesed* to a thousand generations." God's anger or wrath lasts only a short time, while his unfailing love and mercy last forever.

The Greek words most often used for mercy in the New Testament are the verb *eleeō* and the noun *eleos*. Though the word *mercy* is peppered throughout the Old Testament, the New Testament brings it into perfect focus in the life and ministry of Jesus. Wherever Jesus went, he encountered suffering people who cried out for mercy. Mark's Gospel tells the story of one such individual:

> When Bartimaeus heard that Jesus of Nazareth was nearby, he began to shout, "Jesus, Son of David, have mercy on me!"
>
> "Be quiet!" many of the people yelled at him.
>
> But he only shouted louder, "Son of David, have mercy on me!"
>
> MARK 10:47-48

Jesus rewarded Bartimaeus by healing his blindness. And because God is merciful, he expects us to show mercy. In one of his most famous parables, Jesus instructs his listeners about the meaning of mercy by telling the story of the Good Samaritan. While everyone else simply passes by the man who was beaten and robbed, the Samaritan helps him and extends mercy to him (Luke 10:30-37).

Lives that are built on God's mercy will inevitably reflect that mercy to others.

Lord, when you described yourself to Moses, you said you were "filled with unfailing love." Whenever I feel unworthy, help me to picture you filled to the brim with unfailing love for me. Let your mercy draw me close and fill me up so that I can show mercy to others.

Studying His Mercy

1. How have you experienced God's mercy? Be as specific as possible.

2. Have you ever thought that God was angry with you? What were the circumstances? How did it affect you when you thought he was angry?

3. Compare the first two lines of Exodus 34:7 with the remainder of the verse. What is God saying about the nature of his mercy compared to the nature of his judgment?

4. Think for a moment about the phrase *unfailing love*. How would your life change if you were convinced that those two words sum up God's attitude toward you?

5. How has God enabled you to show mercy to others? Are you growing in mercy?

6. Psalm 103:13 says that God is "tender and compassionate to those who fear him." Why do you think the psalmist links the fear of God with expressions of his mercy?

7. Is it possible to make mercy inoperative? If so, how? Take a look at Romans 2:1-11; 11:22 to see what the Bible has to say.

Tuesday

PRAYING IN LIGHT OF GOD'S MERCY

The LORD replied to Moses, "I will indeed do what you have asked, for I look favorably on you, and I know you by name."

Moses responded, "Then show me your glorious presence."

The LORD replied, "I will make all my goodness pass before you, and I will call out my name, Yahweh, before you. For I will show mercy to anyone I choose, and I will show compassion to anyone I choose. But you may not look directly at my face, for no one may see me and live." The LORD continued, "Look, stand near me on this rock. As my glorious presence passes by, I will hide you in the crevice of the rock and cover you with my hand until I have passed by. Then I will remove my hand and let you see me from behind. But my face will not be seen."

EXODUS 33:17-23

Reflect On:	Exodus 33:17-23
Praise God:	For revealing himself to Moses and to us
Offer Thanks:	That one of the first words God uses to describe himself to Moses is *mercy*
Confess:	Your need to embrace God's self-revelation
Ask God:	To give you a sense of his glorious presence

Many people harbor the fear that the God depicted in the Bible suffers from a personality disorder. He seems kind and loving one moment and mean and wrathful the next. It's true that the Bible speaks of God's love and mercy, and it also speaks of his jealousy and judgment.

In a misguided attempt to heal this apparent split in God's

personality, some Christians have cast the God of the Old Testament as the polar opposite of Jesus in the New Testament. Embarrassed or repulsed by depictions that seem to show God in a negative light, they rarely read the Old Testament or they ignore it completely.

One way to tackle the apparent contradictions in God's nature is to look at the relationship between mercy and justice. *Mercy* is a word most of us can easily embrace. It captures God's response toward human misery and the suffering of all creatures. The word *justice*, on the other hand, can sound foreboding, as it refers to God's attitude toward human guilt. But both mercy and justice share the same aim, which is to deal with the soul-destroying power of sin. And both spring from God's goodness and love.

A god who is only merciful would be like an oncologist who refuses to prescribe chemotherapy, radiation, or surgery for fear of inflicting short-term pain on a patient who would otherwise die of cancer. Without justice, God would not be good, loving, or powerful, because he could not address the wrongs we do to ourselves and others.

If you wonder why the Bible sometimes depicts God as angry at faithless Israel, consider the words of Rabbi Abraham Joshua Heschel, who points out that "the wrath of God is a lamentation."[1] This is God's expression of anguish at the way sin has distorted the world he made.

"Is it a sign of cruelty," Heschel asks, "that God's anger is aroused when the rights of the poor are violated, when widows and orphans are oppressed?"[2]

Ultimately, the best way to try to understand God is to interpret the Old Testament in light of the New Testament. Our doubts about God's mercy can be resolved in Jesus, who, as the book of Hebrews affirms, is the exact representation of God's being (1:3).

As finite creatures, we cannot help but misunderstand God. Paul says, "Now we see things imperfectly, like puzzling reflections in a mirror, but then we will see everything with perfect clarity. All that I know now is partial and incomplete, but then I will know everything completely, just as God now knows me completely" (1 Corinthians 13:12). Until then, let's celebrate the truth that Scripture teaches—that God is who he says he is: a God of both justice and mercy, slow to anger, and filled with unfailing love and faithfulness.

Wednesday

PRAYING IN LIGHT OF GOD'S MERCY

> *In all their suffering he also suffered,*
>   *and he personally rescued them.*
> *In his love and mercy he redeemed them.*
>   *He lifted them up and carried them*
>   *through all the years.*

ISAIAH 63:9

> *May God give you more and more mercy, peace, and love.*

JUDE 1:2

Reflect On: Isaiah 63:9; Jude 1:2
Praise God: For showing you his redeeming mercy
Offer Thanks: That Jesus became human to save you
Confess: Any tendency to judge others harshly
Ask God: To give you his heart for others

My youngest is always asking if she can climb into my bed or, failing that, if I might consider sleeping in her room. But since I actually like to sleep at night, I usually decline the invitation. Her fear of the dark reminds me of the tale of a little boy whose father had just tucked him in and turned out the lights.

"Daddy, I'm scared!" the boy cried.

"But, honey," came the reassuring reply, "there's nothing to be afraid of. God loves you, and he'll watch over you."

"Yes, I know God loves me," the boy shot back. "But right now I need somebody with skin on 'em."

When it comes to understanding God's mercy, we need to

remember that he wants people with skin on 'em—people like you and me—to display his mercy to others.

High school athlete Meghan Vogel recently captured Ohio's 1,600 meter title in the Ohio Division III track and field state meet. Later that day she did something even more remarkable. During the 3,200 meter final, she spotted fellow runner Arden McMath collapsed on the track, twenty feet from the finish line. Instead of running past McMath, Vogel stooped down and lifted her onto her feet. The girls ran the rest of the race together arm in arm. Then, just before they crossed the finish line, Vogel stepped back, still holding the other girl up, so McMath could finish ahead of her.

The fans went wild. Later, when asked for her reaction to the crowd's roar of approval, she seemed surprised. She'd been so focused on McMath that she hadn't noticed all the cheering. When people praised her for letting the other girl finish first, she merely replied, "She was ahead of me the whole race; she deserved to finish before me."[3]

Captured on video, Vogel's act of kindness went viral. Her selfless act hit a responsive chord with millions of people who admired what she had done.

It strikes me that the story of these two runners presents a fitting picture of what Christ has done for us, stooping down to lift us up and then staying with us until we are safely across the finish line.

Though most of our good deeds will never be caught on camera, the eyes that matter most are trained on us right now. As Scripture says, "The eyes of the LORD search the whole earth in order to strengthen those whose hearts are fully committed to him" (2 Chronicles 16:9). Let's look for ways to show mercy today.

Thursday

PRAYING IN LIGHT OF GOD'S MERCY

O people, the LORD has told you what is good,
and this is what he requires of you:
to do what is right, to love mercy,
and to walk humbly with your God.

MICAH 6:8

You must be compassionate, just as your Father is compassionate.
Do not judge others, and you will not be judged. Do not condemn
others, or it will all come back against you. Forgive others, and you
will be forgiven.

LUKE 6:36-37

Reflect On: Micah 6:8; Luke 6:36-37
Praise God: For shaping you toward mercy
Offer Thanks: For the way God has shown you compassion
Confess: Any lack of mercy toward others
Ask God: To help you reflect his mercy to others

Genelle Guzman-McMillan worked on the sixty-fourth floor
of the North Tower of the World Trade Center in New York.
When American Airlines flight 11 slammed into the building
on the morning of September 11, 2001, she felt the building
shake. Heeding the advice of the Port Authority Police, she
decided to stay put. But an hour later when panic finally set
in, she began descending the smoke-filled stairway. Sixty-three,
sixty-two, sixty . . . forty-nine, forty-eight, forty-seven. When
she reached the thirteenth floor, pausing to take off her high

226

heels, the North Tower suddenly collapsed in a deafening roar, and everything went black. One hundred and ten floors were coming down around her, burying her alive and trapping her beneath a stairwell.

Pinned beneath a mountain of rubble, her mouth and nose caked with grime, Genelle did the only thing she could think of. She cried out to God, saying, "You've got to help me! . . . Give me a second chance. Please save my life!"[4] Twenty-seven hours later, when rescuers finally discovered her, she became the last survivor of the World Trade Center Towers collapse.

If you were to meet this dark-eyed woman, you would hardly believe all she endured. She looks too healthy, too happy to have suffered what she did. Remarkably, she has never experienced any bitterness toward God for allowing such a tragedy to occur. In fact, when I met her, she stunned me by saying she doesn't regret having been in the building that day because it was when she was buried alive under a mountain of rubble that she came to know the life-giving power of Christ.

Henry Ward Beecher, a nineteenth-century preacher and the brother of Harriet Beecher Stowe, puts the concept of God's severe mercy in rather stark terms: "What has made you so patient?" he asks. "What has made you so broad, so deep, and so rich? God put pickaxes into you, though you did not like it. He dug wells of salvation in you. He took you in His strong hand and shook you by His north wind. He rolled you in His snows and fed you with the coarsest food. He clothed you in the coarsest raiment and beat you as a flail beats grain till the straw is gone and the wheat is left.

"And you are what you are by the grace of God's providence, many of you. By fire, by anvil strokes, by the hammer that breaks the flinty rock, you are made what you are. You were gold in the rock, and God played miner, and blasted you out of the rock."

Beecher goes on to say, "Now you are gold, free from the rock by the grace of God's severity to you. . . . No person is ordained until his sorrows put into his hands the power of comforting others."[5]

Let me make it clear that I don't think God is wielding a divine pickax or a gigantic hammer, though at times it may feel as if he is. Beecher was reaching for vivid imagery to help his listeners grasp hold of an analogy that is supported by Scripture—that God is actively reshaping us into his image. Sometimes he does this by drawing treasure out of our sufferings, turning evil circumstances to a good purpose for those who love him.

"There is wonderful joy ahead," the apostle Peter says, "even though you must endure many trials for a little while. These trials will show that your faith is genuine. It is being tested as fire tests and purifies gold" (1 Peter 1:6-7).

Today, as you ponder God's mercy, ask him to show you how he has already redeemed many of your sorrows, making you into a person who has not only been touched by his mercy but who has also learned to show mercy to others.

Friday

PROMISES ASSOCIATED WITH GOD'S MERCY

Despite what our children might think, most of us don't go out of our way to make their lives miserable when they do something wrong. Because the bedrock of our relationship with them is love, we want to help them. We understand their frailty because we, too, are human—so human that we might even remember how tough it can be to be a kid.

I think that's how our heavenly Father sees us. He responds to our misery with kindness, eager to help when we fail. I find it comforting that the Bible characterizes God's anger as momentary while emphasizing that his mercy endures forever. That's exactly what you would expect of a good father. Mercy, not anger, is built into the fiber of God's being. The Bible tells us many things about the richness of God's mercy, saying that he delights in it and that he is kind, compassionate, and slow to anger.

Our own store of mercy may run out, but God's mercies are new every morning. Let's proclaim the truth today: "The faithful love of the LORD never ends! His mercies never cease" (Lamentations 3:22).

Promises in Scripture

> The faithful love of the LORD never ends!
> His mercies never cease.
> Great is his faithfulness;
> his mercies begin afresh each morning.
>
> LAMENTATIONS 3:22-23

> "The mountains may move
> and the hills disappear,
> but even then my faithful love for you will remain.

229

> My covenant of blessing will never be broken,"
> says the LORD, who has mercy on you.

ISAIAH 54:10

Since we have a great High Priest who has entered heaven, Jesus the Son of God, let us hold firmly to what we believe. This High Priest of ours understands our weaknesses, for he faced all of the same testings we do, yet he did not sin. So let us come boldly to the throne of our gracious God. There we will receive his mercy, and we will find grace to help us when we need it most.

HEBREWS 4:14-16

All praise to God, the Father of our Lord Jesus Christ. God is our merciful Father and the source of all comfort. He comforts us in all our troubles so that we can comfort others. . . . The Lord is full of tenderness and mercy.

2 CORINTHIANS 1:3-4; JAMES 5:11

Continued Prayer and Praise
Psalm 123
Proverbs 28:13
Isaiah 63:7-9
Jeremiah 31:20
Matthew 9:10-13
Matthew 18:21-33
Luke 1:46-50, 76-79
2 Corinthians 1:3-4
Ephesians 2:4-7
1 Timothy 1:16
Titus 3:4-7
James 3:17
1 Peter 2:10
Jude 1:23

14

GOD NEVER GIVES UP

FAITHFUL

His Nature

Faithfulness is in short supply in our world. We know of no one who is capable of acting with complete integrity, nobody who is strong enough to keep every promise he or she has ever made. So it can be difficult to fathom how faithful God is.

But Scripture assures us that God will never abandon those who belong to him. Even when we fail, he is faithful and will forgive us. He never gives up, never loses faith, never breaks a promise. Because God is absolutely steady and reliable and completely true to his nature, we can lean into him, finding rest for our souls as we trust in his great faithfulness.

Key Scripture

> The faithful love of the LORD never ends!
>   His mercies never cease.
> Great is his faithfulness;
>   his mercies begin afresh each morning.
>
> LAMENTATIONS 3:22-23

Monday

GOD REVEALS HIMSELF

The faithful love of the LORD never ends!
    His mercies never cease.
Great is his faithfulness;
    his mercies begin afresh each morning.
I say to myself, "The LORD is my inheritance;
    therefore, I will hope in him!"

LAMENTATIONS 3:22-24

Those who live in the shelter of the Most High
    will find rest in the shadow of the Almighty.
This I declare about the LORD:
He alone is my refuge, my place of safety;
    he is my God, and I trust him.
For he will rescue you from every trap
    and protect you from deadly disease.
He will cover you with his feathers.
    He will shelter you with his wings.
    His faithful promises are your armor and
        protection.
Do not be afraid of the terrors of the night,
    nor the arrow that flies in the day.
Do not dread the disease that stalks in
        darkness,
    nor the disaster that strikes at midday. . . .

If you make the LORD your refuge,
    if you make the Most High your shelter,
no evil will conquer you;
    no plague will come near your home.

PSALM 91:1-6, 9-10

Understanding His Faithfulness

Psalm 91 paints a vivid picture of God's faithfulness. Possessing strength, wisdom, and steadfastness, he is always a place of refuge and safety for believers. He is like an eagle sheltering its young from danger. Because God is faithful, we can proclaim with the psalmist that if we make the Lord our refuge, no evil will conquer us. Though God will not prevent every misfortune, he has promised to protect our souls from evil.

When the Bible says that God is faithful, it means he is also faithful to himself—always acting in ways that are consistent with his nature. Unlike fickle human beings, God never wavers in his love, mercy, justice, holiness, or goodness. Because he is utterly faithful, we can lean on him and trust in him. God's faithfulness is what gives us confidence in his promises. He is our rock, our fortress, a very present help in times of trouble.

What does it mean to take refuge in the Lord? It means first of all that we place our faith in him, trusting that he is who he says he is. But having faith in God involves more than intellectual assent. It demands complete commitment. It requires obedience: we trust God enough to obey him. Disobedience is simply an outward manifestation of unbelief. Instead of trusting God, we trust ourselves to know what is best.

Taking refuge in the Lord means we will seek him first, not last, when trouble comes. It means we will rely on his Word as the truth. It means we will lean into him rather than leaning into our fears or desires. It means we will never attempt to "revise God"—to "remake him" in a way that is either softer or harder than he is.

The Hebrew word 'āman can be translated "believe," "faithful," "trust," "believed," or "trustworthy." The word mûnâ can be translated "faithfulness," "truth," "faithful," or "faithfully" and is often used to refer to God's character, as in Psalm 100: "The LORD is good. His unfailing love continues forever, and his faithfulness continues to each generation" (v. 5).

In the New Testament the word *amēn* is a transliteration of the Hebrew aman. When we say "amen," we are committing ourselves to act in accordance with the truth we have affirmed. As Christ's followers, we are called to be faithful—to refuse to compromise our faith even in the face of persecution.

If you want to know what human faithfulness looks like, consider the life of Paul, a man who suffered greatly because of his love for Christ. He was shipwrecked, imprisoned, beaten, and stoned. Yet instead of giving up, Paul acclaimed God's faithfulness by challenging believers in Rome: "If God is for us, who can ever be against us?" (Romans 8:31). Paul had learned the secret of contentment. He knew how to rest in God's faithfulness, trusting that each morning would bring fresh mercies from the God who loved him.

Lord, you are true to yourself and to the promises you've made. Thank you for never failing or forsaking me. Help me to learn to rest in your faithfulness. Strengthen me so that I might always be faithful to you.

Studying His Faithfulness

1. The passage from Lamentations implies a link between hope and God's faithfulness. How do you think those two ideas are connected?

2. How might your life be different if you lived with the expectation that each morning would bring new mercies from God?

3. What does it mean to "live in the shelter of the Most High" and to "find rest in the shadow of the Almighty"? Give specific examples.

4. Why is it difficult for human beings to comprehend faithfulness?
5. What circumstances challenge your ability to be faithful to God and others?
6. What does the psalmist mean when he says that "no evil will conquer you"? How have you experienced this in your life?

Tuesday

PRAYING IN LIGHT OF GOD'S FAITHFULNESS

There is no one like the God of Israel.
He rides across the heavens to help you,
across the skies in majestic splendor.
The eternal God is your refuge,
and his everlasting arms are under you.

DEUTERONOMY 33:26-27

In that day the remnant left in Israel,
the survivors in the house of Jacob,
will no longer depend on allies
who seek to destroy them.
But they will faithfully trust the LORD,
the Holy One of Israel.

ISAIAH 10:20

Reflect On: Deuteronomy 33:26-27; Isaiah 10:20
Praise God: Because he is true to himself
Offer Thanks: That God is your faithful Father, who will never abandon you
Confess: Your self-reliance
Ask God: To help you to faithfully follow him

I grew up on a large inland lake in Michigan. Entire summers were spent ramming around in a small motorboat pursuing a favorite pastime: turtle hunting. There were tiny painted turtles—my favorites—and giant snapping turtles and every variety of turtle in between.

One sunny afternoon, my older brother stepped out of the boat and onto a sandy patch of ground in a shallow area of the lake. Great hunter that he was, Bob hopped out with his net in hand, in eager pursuit of a turtle he'd just spotted. Suddenly he began flailing, falling backward into the water and letting out a little yelp of fear. It seemed the sandy bottom of the lake had suddenly given way beneath him. Apparently when Bob had climbed out of the boat, he'd mistaken the back of a large soft-shell turtle for the bottom of the lake. The turtle took off, leaving my brother behind.

Those of us watching from the boat were laughing so hard we could hardly breathe. The story of Bob the Great Hunter and Fearless Turtle Warrior has become part of our family lore, eliciting laughter whenever it's retold at family gatherings.

Still, as anyone who has experienced even a mild earthquake will tell you, feeling the earth shift beneath your feet is not very funny. In every life there are seismic shocks—the death of a loved one, economic downturn, divorce, illness. When such crises happen, it can feel as though deep chasms have opened beneath you. The people and things you've always depended on are revealed in all their frailty. What then?

It depends on the foundation that has been built beneath your life. If you have put your hope in God, sooner or later you will experience the truth of his Word, which says, "The eternal God is your refuge, and his everlasting arms are under you" (Deuteronomy 33:27). God will carry you. He will make a way. Even if you face fear and pain and sleepless nights, he will not let you fall.

Wednesday

PRAYING IN LIGHT OF GOD'S FAITHFULNESS

The temptations in your life are no different from what others experience. And God is faithful. He will not allow the temptation to be more than you can stand. When you are tempted, he will show you a way out so that you can endure.

1 CORINTHIANS 10:13

If we confess our sins to him, he is faithful and just to forgive us our sins and to cleanse us from all wickedness.

1 JOHN 1:9

May the God of peace make you holy in every way, and may your whole spirit and soul and body be kept blameless until our Lord Jesus Christ comes again. God will make this happen, for he who calls you is faithful.

1 THESSALONIANS 5:23-24

Reflect On:	1 Corinthians 10:13; 1 John 1:9; 1 Thessalonians 5:23-24
Praise God:	For promising to be faithful to us
Offer Thanks:	That God will not allow you to be defeated if you hope in him
Confess:	Any tendency to give in to hopelessness when life gets difficult
Ask God:	To help you to remain faithful despite the unfaithfulness of others

Sometimes it's easier to explain what faithfulness looks like by conjuring its opposite. Remember Lucy van Pelt, the crabby, bossy little girl who kept snatching the football away just when Charlie Brown was ready to kick it? We laugh as the characters play out the script over and over, wondering how Charlie Brown could possibly fall for Lucy's dastardly trick one more time.

But for some of us, the laughter is bittersweet. We've encountered our own versions of Lucy van Pelt, perhaps in the guise of a spouse who has broken marriage vows or a parent who has abandoned or neglected us. The wounds of faithlessness are many and deep. Some of us experience them repeatedly because something deep within us keeps trying to forge relationships with people who can't seem to keep a promise.

Fortunately, God bears no resemblance to such people. Unlike fickle human beings, God never wavers in his commitments due to boredom, fear, weakness, difficulty, or selfishness. His persevering love sustains us even if we waver in our love for him.

The New Testament tells us of three concrete ways in which God expresses his faithfulness:

- No matter how much we are tempted, God will be faithful in helping us find a way out of temptation (1 Corinthians 10:13).
- If we confess our sins, God is faithful to forgive us and to cleanse us from them (1 John 1:9).
- God will not leave his work in us half completed but will make us holy in every way (1 Thessalonians 5:23-24).

Take a moment to think about that last promise. Paul says that God will make your "whole spirit and soul and body" blameless. That means every part of you will become whole and healthy. You will experience total victory over the deforming power of sin.

Because God is both faithful and creative, he will use everything in your life—even the Lucy van Pelts—to bring you to a place of perfect peace and wholeness. Your life no longer has to be ruled by anguish, insecurity, frustration, depression, or confusion. You don't have to live in fear of letting others down or being let down. Instead, you can experience the joy and peace that come from resting in the faithfulness of God.

Thursday

PRAYING IN LIGHT OF GOD'S FAITHFULNESS

You are blessed because you believed that the Lord would do what he said.

LUKE 1:45

He will keep you strong to the end so that you will be free from all blame on the day when our Lord Jesus Christ returns. God will do this, for he is faithful to do what he says, and he has invited you into partnership with his Son, Jesus Christ our Lord.

1 CORINTHIANS 1:8-9

Reflect On: Luke 1:45; 1 Corinthians 1:8-9
Praise God: For blessing those who remain faithful
Offer Thanks: For God's promise to keep us strong
Confess: Any tendency to distrust God's heart
                toward you
Ask God: To help you rest in his faithfulness

Earlier this year, my elderly mother had to have a PICC line inserted in her upper arm to combat a persistent infection. I held her hand as the nurse specialist performed an ultrasound and then carefully inserted a long, slender tube that made its way into a large vessel leading to her heart.

Suffering from confusion and anxiety, my mother had already pulled out an IV, which had been inserted because she was refusing to swallow pills. The PICC line was more difficult to yank out and provided better delivery of the medicine. Before I left that morning, I did my best to explain why she needed the procedure,

244

even managing to extract a promise that under no circumstances would she think of removing it.

Within three days, the PICC line was gone because my frail-as-a-feather mother had managed to pull it out. Though she finally agreed to a course of oral antibiotics, that experience made me wonder about how many times I fail to receive what I need because I find it difficult to trust God, to believe deep down that he is faithful.

God says he owns the cattle on a thousand hills, and yet I feel anxious about the future. He says he is slow to anger and quick to forgive, and yet I feel as though he is chronically angry because I am less than perfect. He says he longs to be gracious, and yet I anticipate more trouble than blessing.

How would our lives change if we truly understood God's faithfulness? Would we be so frustrated and fearful if we knew that God will never break his promises because he cannot be faithless to himself? Though it's hard to wait for what seems like an intolerably long time to receive his blessings, wouldn't we have more peace if we had complete confidence in God?

Sometimes we impugn God's character by questioning his power and his goodness. Regardless of what we are facing, let's ask him to defeat our anxiety and unbelief. No matter how strong the pressure against faith is, let's refuse to yank out the spiritual PICC line that he has placed in us for our protection.

Trying to live the Christian life without believing in God's faithfulness is like attempting to ride a bicycle without tires or trying to sing a song without a melody. If you find yourself tired and tempted to give up, ask God to give you what you need today—an increase in faith and hope. As you spread your need before him, put whatever faith you do have into believing he will hear and help, remembering that he has promised to keep you strong to the end.

Friday

PROMISES ASSOCIATED WITH GOD'S FAITHFULNESS

Years ago author Barbara Johnson wrote a book entitled *Where Does a Mother Go to Resign?* Barbara's book captures the sense of frustration parents can feel when dealing with significant difficulties in the lives of their children. For some of us, the challenges lie in other areas—perhaps on the job or in our marriages.

Whenever I feel like giving up in the face of intractable problems, I like to reread a story from Scripture that highlights a dangerous moment in Judah's history, when a vast army was headed its way. Though the situation looked hopeless, Judah's king refused to despair. Instead, he gathered his people together and proclaimed a fast. Then he begged God for his help. This is how God answered him: "Do not be afraid! Don't be discouraged by this mighty army, for the battle is not yours, but God's" (2 Chronicles 20:15).

Taking those words to heart, the king exhorted the people, "Listen to me, all you people of Judah and Jerusalem! Believe in the LORD your God, and you will be able to stand firm" (20:20). Another translation says, "Have faith in the LORD your God and you will be upheld" (NIV). The people believed God and rejoiced when he did exactly as he had promised, upholding them by destroying their enemies.

Each of us faces different struggles. My challenges are different from yours. But all of us will at times face the temptation to give up, throw in the towel, say we've had enough. Instead of surrendering to hopelessness, let's keep crying out to God. For if we have faith in him, he will surely uphold us.

Promises in Scripture

God is not a man, so he does not lie.
He is not human, so he does not change his mind.
Has he ever spoken and failed to act?
Has he ever promised and not carried
it through?

NUMBERS 23:19

Listen to me, all you people of Judah and Jerusalem! Believe in the LORD your God, and you will be able to stand firm.

2 CHRONICLES 20:20

Give thanks to the LORD, for he is good!
His faithful love endures forever.
Cry out, "Save us, O God of our salvation!
Gather and rescue us from among the nations,
so we can thank your holy name
and rejoice and praise you."

Praise the LORD, the God of Israel,
who lives from everlasting to everlasting!

And all the people shouted "Amen!" and praised the LORD.

1 CHRONICLES 16:34-36

Jesus Christ, the Son of God, does not waver between "Yes" and "No." He is the one whom Silas, Timothy, and I preached to you, and as God's ultimate "Yes," he always does what he says. For all of God's promises have been fulfilled in Christ with a resounding "Yes!" And through Christ, our "Amen" (which means "Yes") ascends to God for his glory.

2 CORINTHIANS 1:19-20

This is the message from the one who is the Amen—the faithful and true witness, the beginning of God's new creation.

REVELATION 3:14

Continued Prayer and Praise

Deuteronomy 7:9
Isaiah 43:1-20
Habakkuk 2:4
Matthew 25:14-30
Hebrews 2:16-18
Revelation 19:11

GOD IS BETTER THAN ANYONE YOU KNOW

HOLY

His Nature

What does holiness mean? It means that everything about God is infinitely better than the best thing you know about anyone else. Even though God is present in the world he created, he is unique, transcending space and time. His holiness encompasses his absolute purity and goodness. When we come into relationship with God, we encounter profound mystery—a being who cannot be measured or fathomed and who can be known only to the degree he reveals himself.

As Christ's followers, we are transformed rather than destroyed by God's power because Jesus has made it safe for us to come into the presence of a holy God, who cannot tolerate sin. Christ's own holiness has become our bridge into God's presence. His purity is contagious, spreading to us—not because of our inherent goodness, but because we belong to him. As God's holy people, we are called to be different from others in the world around us, dedicated to God and set apart for his service.

Key Scripture

> Holy, holy, holy is the LORD of Heaven's Armies!
> The whole earth is filled with his glory!

ISAIAH 6:3

Monday

GOD REVEALS HIMSELF

It was in the year King Uzziah died that I saw the Lord. He was sitting on a lofty throne, and the train of his robe filled the Temple. Attending him were mighty seraphim, each having six wings. With two wings they covered their faces, with two they covered their feet, and with two they flew. They were calling out to each other,

> "Holy, holy, holy is the LORD of Heaven's Armies!
> The whole earth is filled with his glory!"

Their voices shook the Temple to its foundations, and the entire building was filled with smoke.

Then I said, "It's all over! I am doomed, for I am a sinful man. I have filthy lips, and I live among a people with filthy lips. Yet I have seen the King, the LORD of Heaven's Armies."

Then one of the seraphim flew to me with a burning coal he had taken from the altar with a pair of tongs. He touched my lips with it and said, "See, this coal has touched your lips. Now your guilt is removed, and your sins are forgiven."

ISAIAH 6:1-7

Understanding His Holiness

Holiness is a word that can make us feel uneasy. It seems lofty, threatening, alien. We instinctively sense that God's holiness has dangerous overtones. His purity calls our sinful attachments into question, demanding that we forsake them in order to enjoy the greatest good of all—belonging to a God of infinite love and power. To come casually, with our hearts grasping tightly the sins we cherish, or to come lightly, as though those sins are no big deal, might be like throwing ourselves onto a roaring fire with the expectation we will not perish. How then, can we—sinful and broken human beings—hope to come into the presence of a holy God and survive the experience?

When God was forging a relationship with the Israelites, he told Moses, "Give the following instructions to the entire community of Israel. You must be holy because I, the LORD your God, am holy" (Leviticus 19:2). God was calling his people into relationship with himself, and he wanted his people not only to survive the experience but also to be nourished by it. But for that to happen, they needed to know the ground rules; they needed to come to him on his terms, not theirs.

The Hebrew word for holiness is *qōdes*, a word that highlights the realm of the sacred in contrast to everything common and profane. The adjective *qādôš*, or "holy," refers to God and what belongs to him. In various places in the Hebrew Scriptures, God is called by the title "the Holy One of Israel" (Isaiah 30:15; Ezekiel 39:7).

Time, space, objects, and people—all can become holy if they belong to God. The Temple in Jerusalem was considered holy space, and the objects used in worship were holy objects. The Sabbath days and feasts God instructed the Israelites to observe were considered holy days or seasons. And the Israelites were called God's holy people by virtue of belonging to him (Deuteronomy 7:6).

The New Testament uses the words *hagiazo*, meaning to "make holy," and *hagio*, meaning "holy" or "sacred." Jesus is called "the Holy One of God" (John 6:69). And those who acclaim Jesus as Lord are called *hagioi*, or "saints." As believers, we are literally set apart—made holy—because of our relationship with the one who bridges the gap between a holy God and sinful human beings. But how does Jesus do this?

Remember the legend of King Midas? Everything he touched

turned to gold. Something like that happens when we come into relationship with Christ, the one whose sacrifice healed the rift that sin had created in our relationship with God. Jesus is the one who makes us holy, enabling us to stand in God's presence and join the angels as they sing, "Holy, holy, holy is the LORD."

Lord, I want what you want for me—to be holy, set apart, and different because I no longer belong to this world but to you. Please work your holiness into my life, separating me from whatever holds me back and keeps me from reflecting your character.

Studying His Holiness

1. Why was Isaiah distressed when he found himself in the throne room of God?
2. Isaiah couldn't praise God or proclaim God's message until his lips were purified. What does this symbolic act convey regarding the importance of purity? What are the implications for our own hearts?
3. How has our culture's attitude toward God's holiness changed over the past several decades? What do you think accounts for this shift?
4. Have you ever experienced a sense of awe in God's presence? What were the circumstances?

Tuesday

PRAYING IN LIGHT OF GOD'S HOLINESS

*Holy, holy, holy is the Lord God, the Almighty—
the one who always was, who is, and who is still
to come.*

REVELATION 4:8

Reflect On: Revelation 4
Praise God: For inviting you to come into his holy presence,
                joining the worship that is already underway in
                heaven
Offer Thanks: That God has made a way for you to experience
                his holiness
Confess: Any disregard for his holiness
Ask God: To increase your sense of awe in his presence

Come on, admit it! You're tired of a god who is just a new, improved version of most humans you know. That god might be admirable, but he wouldn't be worth worshiping, and he certainly wouldn't be worth dying for. Because that god would just be a super version of you.

Most of us want to worship a God who is more than just an outstanding person or a great guy. But living as we do in what is arguably the most democratic society in history, it can be easy to lose sight of this perspective. We don't like it when anyone stands out as morally superior. Some of us can't wait for such people to be cut down to size.

Unfortunately, that pattern can persist in our spiritual lives. We like our worship services to be casual so that we can come "just as we are," chewing gum, drinking coffee in the sanctuary, and chatting amiably during the service. God is our friend, after all. Don't get me wrong—I'm a fan of casual. And I believe Jesus is the best friend I will ever have. It's just that an overly casual attitude doesn't help us experience the proper kind of awe in the presence of a God of unimaginable holiness.

Annie Dillard says that most people don't have a clue about the kind of power they're invoking when they pray. Why, she asks, are people wearing fancy hats to church when "we should all be wearing crash helmets?"[1] Do we really believe that we are in the presence of God Almighty, in whom there is no flaw or imperfection?

The Jewish people have developed various ways of reminding themselves of God's holiness. In rabbinic Judaism, Scripture is considered holy, and reading it a sacred act. Writing the scrolls is also considered holy, which is why those who do so must wash their hands afterward. This is one small example of how they celebrate the sacredness of worship through concrete acts and objects.

What if we, too, were to build more tangible signs of God's holiness into our own times of prayer and worship? We might do this by creating beautiful sanctuaries, lighting a few candles, holding the Bible reverently, reading it carefully, and choosing songs that emphasize God's holiness and majesty. Let's ask God to remind us of his holiness so that we might come into his presence in a way that brings him honor and praise.

Wednesday

PRAYING IN LIGHT OF GOD'S HOLINESS

The LORD also said to Moses, "Give the following instructions to the entire community of Israel. You must be holy because I, the LORD your God, am holy."

LEVITICUS 19:1-2

Reflect On: Leviticus 19:1-4, 9-18
Praise God: For showing you how to be holy
Offer Thanks: For the dignity you have as his child
Confess: Your need for grace
Ask God: To give you the courage to be different
                    when different is good

I am not a fan of bumper stickers, particularly the kind that carry political messages. Nor do I like clothing that sports slogans, no matter how cute, true, or insightful they might be. I simply don't like stamping myself with a label. Little wonder, then, that even as a graduate of the University of Michigan, I was able to resist the temptation to buy a T-shirt emblazoned with these words: *Harvard: the Michigan of the East.*

Despite my aversion to labeling, perhaps I should allow at least one exception. What if I had the guts to wear a T-shirt that said *Holy?* Okay, some people would think I was a weird religious nut. But wearing a shirt like that might also make me more aware of my position in Christ and my responsibility to try to reflect his character. It might also make me aware of what is already true—that the way I conduct myself in public and private has a bearing on what people think of the God I profess to love.

A. W. Tozer says, "We tend by a secret law of the soul to move toward our mental image of God."[2] As Christians, we are at least partially responsible for the mental image others form about the God we follow.

What does holy look like? Listen to how God reveals himself to Moses in one of the most sacred scenes from the Old Testament. Moses has just asked him to show him his glory.

The LORD passed in front of Moses, calling out,

> "Yahweh! The LORD!
>   The God of compassion and mercy!
> I am slow to anger
>   and filled with unfailing love and faithfulness."
>
> EXODUS 34:6

A God of compassion and mercy—and yes, justice, righteousness, goodness, and love. He is the God we call holy.

Thursday

PRAYING IN LIGHT OF GOD'S HOLINESS

The high and lofty one who lives in eternity,
the Holy One, says this:
"I live in the high and holy place
with those whose spirits are contrite and humble.
I restore the crushed spirit of the humble
and revive the courage of those with repentant
hearts."

ISAIAH 57:15

Reflect On: Isaiah 57:15
Praise God: Because he revives the humble
Offer Thanks: Because God is close to those who are crushed in spirit
Confess: Your brokenness and your need for God's grace to daily sustain you
Ask God: To help you draw near to him, especially when you are in need of forgiveness and healing

Some people have a problem with the concept of God's holiness because they feel worthless. Talking about how holy and perfect God is makes them want to hide because they are painfully aware of their own failings.

Some of us are so beaten down by life that we walk with shoulders hunched, head bowed. Most of us aren't that obvious. We're good at hiding, masters in the art of pretending. But no matter how well we dress or how confident we look, we still can't shake the shame we feel.

Where does all that shame come from? From children who were mean to us when we were growing up, from abusive or negligent adults, from cultural messages that tell us we're stupid, awkward, weak—from a thousand different sources over the course of our lives. And then there's Satan, who is always eager to reinforce a hurtful message. Like sponges, we absorb these negative ideas about ourselves until they define who we are.

Other times our shame comes from things we've done. We may have cheated or lied or stolen or slept around. We may be addicted to drugs, alcohol, or pornography. Or we may be abusive, angry, or deceitful. We want to change, but we don't know how.

Remember the story in Scripture of the man with leprosy? In ancient times, those with skin diseases had to call out, "Unclean! Unclean!" wherever they went to give others a chance to distance themselves (Leviticus 13:45). But listen to what happened when Jesus encountered a man with leprosy—an outcast who begged for Jesus' cleansing touch. Jesus stretched out his hand, touched the man no one else would touch, and healed him (Matthew 8:2-3).

When we are mired in sin or shame, we tend to feel like an outcast—as though we're not fit for God's company. But for those of us who believe in God, his holiness, rather than our weakness, is what defines the relationship. Indeed, his holiness is contagious—working its way into our lives the more we make it our aim to follow him.

The next time you feel incapable of entering the presence of a holy God, come humbly, asking him to touch and transform you, for he is your Redeemer, the Holy One of Israel.

Friday

PROMISES ASSOCIATED WITH GOD'S HOLINESS

If you want to know what holiness looks like, take a look at the picture Jesus paints in the Beatitudes. The English word *beatitude* means "blessedness" and comes from the Latin word *beatitudo*. Found in Matthew 5:3-12, each of the Beatitudes begins with words that are often translated "Blessed are." And who precisely are blessed? It's not the rich, the well fed, or the successful, as we might think, but those who are poor in spirit, those who mourn, those who hunger and thirst for righteousness. The list Jesus presents in the Sermon on the Mount turns our ideas of blessing upside down, revealing a God who cherishes a heart that is shaped like his. If we want to be holy, we need to adopt the values of the Kingdom Jesus proclaimed.

Theologian John Stott says, "No comment could be more hurtful to the Christian than the words 'But you are no different from anybody else.' For the essential theme of the whole Bible from beginning to end is that God's historical purpose is to call out a people for himself. This people is a 'holy' people, set apart from the world to belong to him and to obey him; its vocation is to be true to its identity, that is, to be 'holy' or 'different' in all its outlook and behavior."[3]

The Beatitudes represent a different kind of life—the life of the person who is transformed by Christ, the one who has made his peace with a holy God.

Promises in Scripture

> God blesses those who are poor and realize
> > their need for him,
> for the Kingdom of Heaven is theirs.
> God blesses those who mourn,
> > for they will be comforted.
> God blesses those who are humble,
> > for they will inherit the whole earth.
> God blesses those who hunger and thirst
> > for justice,
> > for they will be satisfied.
> God blesses those who are merciful,
> > for they will be shown mercy.
> God blesses those whose hearts are pure,
> > for they will see God.
> God blesses those who work for peace,
> > for they will be called the children
> > of God.
> God blesses those who are persecuted for
> > doing right,
> > for the Kingdom of Heaven is theirs.

God blesses you when people mock you and persecute you and lie about you and say all sorts of evil things against you because you are my followers. Be happy about it! Be very glad! For a great reward awaits you in heaven. And remember, the ancient prophets were persecuted in the same way.

MATTHEW 5:3-12

Continued Prayer and Praise

Exodus 15:11
Exodus 39:1, 30
Psalm 29:2
Isaiah 1:4
Isaiah 10:17
Luke 1:35
John 6:69
Acts 2:1-21
1 Corinthians 1:2
2 Corinthians 7:1
1 Peter 1:2, 15-16

16

GOD IS
AN ARTIST

CREATIVE

His Nature

The first thing we learn about God from the Bible is that he is the Creator, the one who makes everything from nothing. After each phase of creation—light, sky, land, animals, plants, and humans—God stops for a moment to survey his work with delight, calling it "good" and finally "very good." Genesis 1 paints the picture of an all-powerful Creator who, simply by speaking, calls a lush, abundant world into being.

Key Scripture

In the beginning God created the heavens and the earth. . . . Then God looked over all he had made, and he saw that it was very good!

GENESIS 1:1, 31

Monday

GOD REVEALS HIMSELF

In the beginning God created the heavens and the earth. The earth was formless and empty, and darkness covered the deep waters. And the Spirit of God was hovering over the surface of the waters.

Then God said, "Let there be light," and there was light. And God saw that the light was good. . . .

Then God said, "Let there be a space between the waters, to separate the waters of the heavens from the waters of the earth." . . . God called the space "sky." . . .

Then God said, "Let the waters beneath the sky flow together into one place, so dry ground may appear." . . . God called the dry ground "land" and the waters "seas." And God saw that it was good. Then God said, "Let the land sprout with vegetation—every sort of seed-bearing plant, and trees that grow seed-bearing fruit." . . .

Then God said, "Let lights appear in the sky to separate the day from the night." . . .

Then God said, "Let the waters swarm with fish and other life. Let the skies be filled with birds of every kind." . . .

Then God said, "Let the earth produce every sort of animal, each producing offspring of the same kind—livestock, small animals that scurry along the ground, and wild animals." . . .

Then God said, "Let us make human beings in our image, to be like us. They will reign over the fish in the sea, the birds in the sky, the livestock, all the wild animals on the earth, and the small animals that scurry along the ground."

> So God created human beings in his own image.
> In the image of God he created them;
> male and female he created them.

Then God blessed them and said, "Be fruitful and multiply. Fill the earth and govern it. Reign over the fish in the sea, the birds in the sky, and all the animals that scurry along the ground." . . .

Then God looked over all he had made, and he saw that it was very good!

GENESIS 1 (SELECTED VERSES)

Understanding His Creativity

Everything that exists owes its existence to God, who is the only being capable of creating something from nothing. Genesis 1 and 2 both tell the story of Creation—but from two different points of view. The first chapter paints the big picture of Creation from God's perspective, while the second focuses primarily on the creation of human beings. Though neither provides a scientific explanation of the origins of the universe, both affirm that the universe owes its existence to God. Genesis paints human beings as the crown of creation, stating that we are made in the image of God.

Psalm 19:1 tells us that "the heavens declare the glory of God" (NIV), and Romans 1:20 points to the fact that through the created world, everyone "can clearly see his invisible qualities—his eternal power and divine nature," leaving us with no excuse for ignorance about God.

Scripture also tells us that God's perfect world was soon corrupted by sin. Rather than abandon it to decay, God promised to create a new heaven and a new earth. God's creative work does not end with the first two chapters of Genesis but continues as he upholds the universe through his constant provision and as he works to bring about the new creation through the advancing reign of his Son.

In the Hebrew Scriptures, the verb *bārā'* means "to create" and is used exclusively to refer to God, who creates a world that cannot exist apart from his sustaining power. Because God created everything, the universe and all that is in it belong to him.

In the New Testament, the verb *ktizō* is used exclusively to describe God's creative activity. Through the agency of Christ, believers are made into new creations (2 Corinthians 5:17).

From Genesis to Revelation, we see the artistry of God at work as he uses his creative power to bring the world into being and then to creatively achieve his purposes.

Lord, thank you for creating human beings in your image. Even though creation has been marred by sin, it still reflects your glory. Help us to recognize this beautiful world as evidence of your love and provision. May we reject the temptation to think of the world as a place to be exploited for our gain, and may we instead accept the call of stewardship as a sacred trust.

Studying His Creative Nature

1. Read Genesis 1 and count how many times God evaluates his creation, proclaiming it good. What does this indicate about his attitude toward everything he has made? How can you reflect that attitude in your own life?
2. How does Genesis 1 reveal God's provision for the world he created?
3. What do you think it means to be created in God's image?
4. What are the practical implications of God's call for us to be stewards—first regarding human life and then regarding the rest of the created world?

5. Think about the miracles Jesus performed while he was on earth. What do they tell us about God's creative power? What do they foretell about the new heaven and the new earth God has promised?
6. How does human creativity relate to God's creative nature?

Tuesday

PRAYING IN LIGHT OF GOD'S CREATIVITY

God saved you by his grace when you believed. And you can't take credit for this; it is a gift from God. Salvation is not a reward for the good things we have done, so none of us can boast about it. For we are God's masterpiece. He has created us anew in Christ Jesus, so we can do the good things he planned for us long ago.

EPHESIANS 2:8-10

I am certain that God, who began the good work within you, will continue his work until it is finally finished on the day when Christ Jesus returns.

PHILIPPIANS 1:6

Reflect On: Ephesians 2:8-10; Philippians 1:6
Praise God: For creating you anew in Jesus Christ
Offer Thanks: Because you are a work in progress
Confess: Your need to see yourself through God's eyes
Ask God: To give you a clearer vision of who you are
              in Christ

I have a neighbor who collects fine art. Chris has made some judicious purchases over the years. Instead of buying a flat-screen TV or golf clubs, he'd rather purchase something beautiful to hang on his walls. This year he decided on an outdoor sculpture from an artist whose work he has admired for many years. On the morning it was delivered, Chris invited me to watch as it was installed in his garden.

273

I was delighted by the invitation, especially since the sculptor was a friend I hadn't seen in many years. I watched as John Merigian and his two sons carefully unloaded the sculpture from a flatbed trailer and then transported it across the lawn. They placed the tall, angular sculpture in the middle of a lush garden bed, its thin shape rising high above the ornamental grasses. The sculpture has so much personality that Chris asked if it had a name.

"*Contender*," came John's reply.

That sounded perfect for the giant, rust-colored figure that looked as though he were striding purposely toward somewhere important.

A few days ago, when I asked how "Skinny Man" was doing (my name for the piece), Chris reminded me that his name is *Contender*. He went on to say that since the sculptor is a religious man, *Contender* must stand for Jacob, who wrestled all night with God (Genesis 32).

These days I find myself looking forward to the first snowfall, wondering how *Contender* will look as the flakes begin to arrange themselves into little drifts on his ledges and angles. That's part of the delight of his shape, which is best enjoyed by observing the interplay between nature and art.

Here's how the artist's website explains his works: "Their complexity lies in the relationships that emerge with the space, lines, silhouettes, shadows, and each other. . . . The movement of the sun across the sculptures through the day is an integral part of creating constantly changing linear elements. Night lighting adds yet another level of variation. Finally, the element of snow in climates where it is present further enhances the linear and geometrical aspects of the sculptures."[1]

It strikes me that John's work hints at the way God acts in our own lives. As Paul says, "We are God's masterpiece. He has created us anew in Christ Jesus, so we can do the good things he planned for us long ago" (Ephesians 2:10). Like the biblical Jacob, we become who we are by virtue of our interactions with God and the world he has made. God has fashioned us into his likeness, using both shadows and light to highlight his work within us so that we can reflect his image to the world.

Wednesday

PRAYING IN LIGHT OF GOD'S CREATIVITY

I am about to do something new.
   See, I have already begun! Do you not see it?
I will make a pathway through the wilderness.
   I will create rivers in the dry wasteland.

ISAIAH 43:19

Reflect On: Isaiah 43:19
Praise God: Because he uses our trials for good
Offer Thanks: Because God's creative work continues today
Confess: Any tendency to doubt God's love when life
             is hard
Ask God: To stop at nothing to make you the person he
             wants you to be

Author and journalist Thomas Friedman has a consistent answer when anyone asks him to name his favorite country. Taiwan, he always says. But why?

"Because Taiwan is a barren rock in a typhoon-laden sea," he explains, "with no natural resources to live off of—it even has to import sand and gravel from China for construction—yet it has the fourth-largest financial reserves in the world."[2]

Friedman's point is that with few natural resources to rely on, the Taiwanese have been forced to invest in the one renewable resource they do have—their people. They have poured their capital into developing a culture and an educational system that enable them to succeed as a nation.

To bolster the notion that a country's success often develops in indirect proportion to its supply of natural resources, Friedman cites a recent study indicating a negative correlation between a country's ability to extract wealth from natural resources and the achievement scores of its high school students.

The overseer of the standardized exams in this study made this intriguing remark: "As the Bible notes, Moses arduously led the Jews for forty years through the desert—just to bring them to the only country in the Middle East that had no oil. But Moses may have gotten it right, after all. Today, Israel has one of the most innovative economies, and its population enjoys a standard of living most of the oil-rich countries in the region are not able to offer."[3]

What does any of this have to do with God's creativity, his ability to bring something out of nothing? Though God has unlimited resources with which to bless his people, his aim isn't to make our lives easy but to make our lives good. He certainly could snap his fingers and solve all our problems, which would make following God feel like winning the lottery. But life with God rarely feels like that.

Instead of handing us one easy win after another, he builds virtue within us by using our circumstances to make us stronger. That's why Paul could encourage the Romans with these words: "We can rejoice, too, when we run into problems and trials, for we know that they help us develop endurance. And endurance develops strength of character, and character strengthens our confident hope of salvation" (Romans 5:3-4).

God does his most creative work within the hearts of those who belong to him, transforming our difficulties into tools he can use for our growth.

What problems are you facing right now? Ask the God who made you to use his creative power to advance his work within you.

Thursday

PRAYING IN LIGHT OF GOD'S CREATIVITY

When I look at the night sky and see the work of
*   your fingers—*
*   the moon and the stars you set in place—*
what are mere mortals that you should think
*   about them,*
*   human beings that you should care for them?*
Yet you made them only a little lower than God
*   and crowned them with glory and honor.*
You gave them charge of everything you made,
*   putting all things under their authority—*
*   the flocks and the herds*
*   and all the wild animals,*
*   the birds in the sky, the fish in the sea,*
*   and everything that swims the ocean currents.*

PSALM 8:3-8

All creation is waiting eagerly for that future day when God will reveal who his children really are. Against its will, all creation was subjected to God's curse. But with eager hope, the creation looks forward to the day when it will join God's children in glorious freedom from death and decay. For we know that all creation has been groaning as in the pains of childbirth right up to the present time.

ROMANS 8:19-22

Reflect On: Psalm 8; Romans 8:19-22
Praise God: Because he has promised to free the world
                from death and decay
Offer Thanks: That God has called us to be his stewards
                on earth

Confess: Any insensitivity to the pain of God's creatures

Ask God: To give you wisdom about the part he wants you to play in taking care of creation

Several years ago I purchased a piano, fulfilling one of my childhood dreams. I took lessons for a few months, but after making little progress, I decided I was no longer interested. Though the piano became nothing but a lovely piece of furniture, I never regretted the purchase. Here's why.

Two years after splurging on the piano, I adopted my first child. I had no way of knowing that this baby would eventually show signs of a prodigious gift. When Katie was four, she started playing the piano, and by the time she was seven, she was spontaneously creating beautiful compositions of her own. Clearly, the piano had been meant for her.

Creativity is highly prized in our culture—and for good reason. But as wonderful as human creativity is, it is still derivative and limited. Though God is good at making something out of nothing, human beings *need something to make something.* We have to use existing materials like paint, canvas, musical instruments, and words to display our artistry.

Though no one questions an artist's rights to his or her work, we often think differently about the things God has made. We pay lip service to the beauty of creation but forget that all of it belongs to God and that he has called humans to be his stewards, caring for the earth as his representatives.

Consider how animals are routinely abused on large corporate farms to maximize profits. Or think about excessive consumerism, which leads to tremendous waste and unsustainable lifestyles.

There is a wonderful dignity in our calling to care for the

earth. As Christians we should embrace this calling by acting wisely on behalf of endangered species and by advocating sound policies to protect forests, clean air, and water.

Surely the systematic abuse of God's creation can't be pleasing to the one who, in Genesis 1, repeated after each phase of his creative work:

"It is good."

"It is good."

"It is good."

If we accept the role God is calling us to play as stewards of creation, he may one day say of our work on earth, "It is good." "It is good." "It is good."

Friday

PROMISES ASSOCIATED WITH GOD'S CREATIVITY

Regardless of whether you are the world's greatest artist or its most inventive thinker, you can still tap into the creative power of God. His creativity did not cease in Genesis but continues in the work of his Son and through the dynamic power of his Spirit. Just as God provides for the physical universe, which is dependent on him for its continued existence, so too does he provide for all who belong to him.

How can you say, then, that the Lord does not see your troubles? Haven't you understood that the Lord is the Creator of all the earth, and that he never grows weak or weary? Trust in the Lord, drawing your strength from his energy, for he can show you how to run without growing weary, to walk and not to faint.

Promises in Scripture

> When you give them your breath,
>   life is created,
>   and you renew the face of the earth.

PSALM 104:30

> O Jacob, how can you say the LORD
>   does not see your troubles?
> O Israel, how can you say God
>   ignores your rights?
> Have you never heard?
>   Have you never understood?
> The LORD is the everlasting God,
>   the Creator of all the earth.

He never grows weak or weary.
　No one can measure the depths of his
　　understanding. . . .
Those who trust in the LORD will find new strength.
　They will soar high on wings like eagles.
They will run and not grow weary.
　They will walk and not faint.

ISAIAH 40:27-28, 31

Look! I am creating new heavens and a new earth,
　and no one will even think about the old ones
　　anymore.
Be glad; rejoice forever in my creation!
　And look! I will create Jerusalem as a place
　　of happiness.
　Her people will be a source of joy. . . .
No longer will babies die when only a few days old.
　No longer will adults die before they have lived
　　a full life.
No longer will people be considered old at one hundred!
　Only the cursed will die that young!
In those days people will live in the houses they build
　and eat the fruit of their own vineyards. . . .
They will not work in vain,
　and their children will not be doomed to
　　misfortune.
For they are people blessed by the LORD,
　and their children, too, will be blessed.
I will answer them before they even call to me.
　While they are still talking about their needs,
　I will go ahead and answer their prayers!

ISAIAH 65:17-18, 20-21, 23-24

Anyone who belongs to Christ has become a new person. The old life is gone; a new life has begun!

2 CORINTHIANS 5:17

Continued Prayer and Praise

Genesis 2:4-25
Psalm 148:3-6
John 1:1-5
Romans 1:20
Romans 4:17
2 Corinthians 5:17
Ephesians 4:24
Colossians 1:15-20
2 Peter 3:10-14
Revelation 21:1

17

GOD IS
ABOVE IT ALL

TRANSCENDENT

His Nature

To say that God exists apart from the universe he created is to invoke a mystery we cannot fathom. It is to admit that he is further above us than we are above the simplest one-celled animals on earth. Utterly independent of the material universe, he exists beyond the range of our perceptions. In his greatness, God exceeds our limitations, our world, our universe. He surpasses our experience, our understanding, and our expectations.

Even though we were made in the image of God, he is not simply a higher and better version of ourselves. He is supreme, preeminent, transcendent, and ultimately mysterious.

Key Scripture

> "Am I a God who is only close at hand?" says the
> LORD.
> "No, I am far away at the same time."
>
> JEREMIAH 23:23

Monday

GOD REVEALS HIMSELF

In the beginning God created the heavens and the earth. The earth was formless and empty, and darkness covered the deep waters. And the Spirit of God was hovering over the surface of the waters.

GENESIS 1:1-2

It was in the year King Uzziah died that I saw the Lord. He was sitting on a lofty throne, and the train of his robe filled the Temple. Attending him were mighty seraphim, each having six wings. With two wings they covered their faces, with two they covered their feet, and with two they flew. They were calling out to each other,

"Holy, holy, holy is the LORD of Heaven's Armies!
The whole earth is filled with his glory!"

Their voices shook the Temple to its foundations, and the entire building was filled with smoke.

Then I said, "It's all over! I am doomed, for I am a sinful man. I have filthy lips, and I live among a people with filthy lips. Yet I have seen the King, the LORD of Heaven's Armies."

ISAIAH 6:1-5

"Am I a God who is only close at hand?" says
the LORD.
"No, I am far away at the same time.
Can anyone hide from me in a secret place?
Am I not everywhere in all the heavens
and earth?"
says the LORD.

JEREMIAH 23:23-24

289

Understanding His Transcendence

As with all of God's attributes, there is irony in attempting to understand God's transcendence. It is his transcendence that makes him so mysterious to human minds. Even so, we can learn about God by taking a closer look at this attribute.

God's transcendence means that he rises above everything and everyone—not necessarily physically, but in terms of quality. Because we tend to think in terms of physical dimensions, the Bible often expresses God's transcendence by telling us that he is high and lofty or that he is exalted. Perhaps that's why many of us can't shake the notion that heaven is "up." Like God, heaven is beyond the limits of our experience. It is part of the supernatural world, which our natural minds cannot conceive.

Whenever God reveals himself to people in the Bible, they are filled with a sense of awe coupled with a profound understanding of their unworthiness. As never before, they see their unlikeness to God. The prophet Isaiah was so overwhelmed by the holiness of God that he was certain he would die (Isaiah 6). Moses covered his face in fear when he encountered God in the form of a burning bush (Exodus 3).

Unfortunately, this sense of God's transcendence is rare in most churches today. Because some of us have grown up in religious environments that instilled a cowering, unhealthy brand of fear, the pendulum has now swung so far in the opposite direction that it's difficult to speak of fear and God in the same sentence without being misunderstood.

But without proper fear for our transcendent God, we will never know the full wonder of belonging to him. Instead, we will continue to underestimate him, letting unbelief erode our confidence in him. Tragically, if we don't learn how to fear God, we will fear everything else. That's why Proverbs 14:27 says, "Fear of the LORD is a life-giving fountain."

Lord, there is no one who can fathom your understanding or contend with your power, no one who can stand against you. Your thoughts are high above mine. Help me to see you as you are and to bow down in your holy presence. I love you, Lord.

Studying His Transcendence

1. What does the passage from Genesis tell us about God's transcendence?
2. Take a moment to prayerfully read Isaiah 6:1-5. Imagine that you are Isaiah and that you have been caught up into God's presence. What would you learn about God and about yourself?
3. How can God be both present and far away, as Jeremiah says?
4. What do you think it means to fear God?
5. How should healthy fear operate in the life of a Christian? How does fear operate in your own life?

Tuesday

PRAYING IN LIGHT OF GOD'S TRANSCENDENCE

I cry out to God Most High,
*   to God who will fulfill his purpose for me.*
He will send help from heaven to rescue me,
*   disgracing those who hound me.*

My God will send forth his unfailing love and
*   faithfulness. . . .*

Be exalted, O God, above the highest heavens.
*   May your glory shine over all the earth.*

PSALM 57:2-3, 11

The high and lofty one who lives in eternity,
*   the Holy One, says this:*
"I live in the high and holy place
*   with those whose spirits are contrite*
*   and humble.*
I restore the crushed spirit of the humble
*   and revive the courage of those with*
*   repentant hearts."*

ISAIAH 57:15

Reflect On:	Psalm 57:2-3, 11; Isaiah 57:15
Praise God:	For being higher than any challenge or problem you face
Offer Thanks:	That God Most High calls you his child
Confess:	Your need for greater humility
Ask God:	To make your prayers powerful

I've been praying for most of my life. Prayers for healing, rescue, relief, repentance, provision, salvation, wisdom, success, deliverance, mercy, forgiveness, patience, and peace. I've prayed for old people, infants, mothers, fathers, physicians, politicians, criminals, teenagers, neighbors, celebrities, pastors, soldiers, nurses, clerks, and folks who've knocked on my door asking for a handout. If you could string my prayers together, they might form a cord long enough to stretch from Earth to Neptune, the farthest planet in our solar system. Truly I have prayed a lot of prayers, and probably so have you.

But for prayers to be effective, they have to reach a destination much farther than the expanse of our solar system. Our prayers have to rise to the ear of the one Scripture describes as the "high and lofty one who lives in eternity." The prophet Isaiah paints a picture of a God who is transcendent, who is enthroned above it all. But in the same breath he says something rather startling—that this majestic God is close to "those whose spirits are contrite and humble."

I was struck by a photo I saw recently of a young Asian boy sitting cross-legged on the ground. His back is to the camera, and he is whispering reverently into a giant ear belonging to a statue of a reclining Buddha. That photo made me think of the universal desire we humans have to pray, to ask for the help of someone bigger than ourselves. Isaiah, of course, would have had no dealings with Buddha, reclining or otherwise. The prophet pictures instead a great and magnificent God who draws near to the lowly and contrite.

One of God's titles in the Hebrew Scriptures is *El Elyon*, God Most High. He is the exalted one, highest in every realm of life. In the New Testament Jesus is called the "Son of the Most High"

(Luke 1:32), while the Holy Spirit is described as the "power of the Most High" (Luke 1:35). Jesus himself tells us that in order to become "children of the Most High," we must act as though we are the most low—lending without expecting something in return, doing good to others, being kind and merciful both to the ungrateful and the wicked (Luke 6:35). Why? Because that's how the Most High God conducts his business.

The great paradox of prayer is that an attitude of lowliness has the power to put us in touch with the most exalted being in the universe. As someone once said, "We stand tallest on our knees"—able to touch heaven through our prayers.

Wednesday

PRAYING IN LIGHT OF GOD'S TRANSCENDENCE

"My thoughts are nothing like your thoughts,"
  says the LORD.
  "And my ways are far beyond anything you
    could imagine.
For just as the heavens are higher than the earth,
  so my ways are higher than your ways
  and my thoughts higher than your thoughts."

ISAIAH 55:8-9

Reflect On: Isaiah 55:8-9
Praise God: For the greatness of his being
Offer Thanks: For his willingness to stoop to our level
Confess: Any disrespect for God expressed through
      your speech or actions
Ask God: To fill you with a sense of holy awe

In the constellation of Cancer, scientists recently discovered a planet, twice the size of ours, which they inelegantly named 55 Cancri e. The remarkable thing about this swiftly moving planet is not its enormous mass (eight times that of Earth's) but that a third of it is made of pure diamond.

The only difficulty for would-be treasure hunters is that this fabulous trove is located 230 trillion miles from Earth, with temperatures that soar to 3,900 degrees Fahrenheit. Even if they could find a way to haul the diamond planet home and cool it down, where would they find a warehouse big enough to store it or enough diamond cutters to slice it into faceted gems?

Yale researcher Nikku Madhusudhan commented on the find: "This is our first glimpse of a rocky world with a fundamentally different chemistry from Earth." We can no longer assume that other rocky planets share the same "chemical constituents, interiors, atmospheres, or biologies" as Earth.[1] As another report explained, "The revelation of the planet's diamond nature means that it could have very different thermal evolution and plate tectonics processes than Earth, which could create bizarre types of volcanism, seismic activity, and mountain formation."[2]

Diamond planets are just one reminder of the many mysteries that remain in the universe. Though each new discovery enhances our understanding, there are still countless things we don't comprehend. It would be safe to say that we don't understand how many things we don't understand.

That's also true when it comes to our knowledge of God. No matter how much we pray or how much we study, he remains a mystery—a being who must always be approached with fear and awe, even by those most confident of his love. Our thoughts are not his thoughts. Our ways are not his ways. He is higher than anything we can imagine.

As we learn about God's attributes, let's ask him to increase our sense of holy fear, remembering that "fear of the LORD is the foundation of wisdom" (Proverbs 9:10). The Bible tells us that fear of God produces many wonderful benefits, including friendship with God, protection from evil, a long life, riches, honor, and salvation. Odd as it may seem, Scripture indicates that the fear of God is a treasure we should seek.

Thursday

PRAYING IN LIGHT OF GOD'S TRANSCENDENCE

Yours, O LORD, is the greatness, the power, the glory, the victory, and the majesty. Everything in the heavens and on earth is yours, O LORD, and this is your kingdom. We adore you as the one who is over all things.

1 CHRONICLES 29:11

What is the price of two sparrows—one copper coin? But not a single sparrow can fall to the ground without your Father knowing it.

MATTHEW 10:29

Reflect On: 1 Chronicles 29:11; Matthew 10:29
Praise God: For his greatness
Offer Thanks: That God has given you a glimpse of his majesty
Confess: Any tendency to limit God
Ask God: To help you see how big he is

Wen Jiabao, prime minister of China, comes from a family that has managed to amass a fortune of at least $2.7 billion. Sebastián Piñera, president of Chile, has an estimated net worth of $2.4 billion. Vladimir Putin, president of Russia, is said (by his enemies) to have accumulated more than $40 billion while in office. Closer to home, the average US senator is worth nearly $8 million. Barack Obama has a net worth of between $1.6 and $7.7 million. With so much money padding their lives, how can wealthy politicians begin to understand the problems of ordinary citizens? Are they in danger of becoming like the Chinese emperor who, upon being informed that his subjects didn't have enough rice to eat, responded by saying, "Why don't they eat meat?"[3]

You might wonder whether the transcendent God is like some out-of-touch politician who can't see the trees for the forest. Is he looking down at the world from thirty thousand feet, aware of the big picture but clueless about the details of people's lives—the place most of us live? How can God both transcend our world and be present within the creation he has made?

Consider this: though God is transcendent, existing beyond the material world, he is also infinite. That means he is a God to whom physical boundaries mean nothing. It's impossible to limit God to the confines of the universe, but neither can you exclude him from it. He is present everywhere.

The Bible assures us that our big God is not too big to care about the smallest details of our lives. Perhaps it is true to say that the only place in the whole wide world from which God can be excluded is within the confines of our hearts. He waits for us to invite him in.

Let's do that today as we proclaim that greatness, power, glory, majesty, and victory belong to him forever.

Friday

PROMISES ASSOCIATED WITH GOD'S TRANSCENDENCE

Have you ever seen small children sheltering behind their parents, clutching onto pant legs as they peek out from behind? That's a little like the picture Psalm 91:1 paints of God's people as it promises protection to those who "live in the shelter of the Most High" or "in the shelter of *Elyon.*"

The setting for the psalm is the Temple in Jerusalem. Because God chose to dwell there, the Jewish people considered the Temple the place in which heaven and earth intersected. The psalmist recognized that the safest place to be is in the sheltering presence of the Most High.

History tells us that only God, whose power extends beyond earth, is capable of protecting us from all the evils that threaten. Though God may not shield us from physical evils, we can be confident that he will always protect us from the evils that threaten to destroy our souls. As Charles Spurgeon once remarked, "It is impossible that any ill should happen to the man who is beloved of the Lord. . . . Ill to him is no ill, but only good in a mysterious form."[4]

The next time you are afraid, pray through Psalm 91. Instead of obsessing over your fears, take a moment to move into God's sheltering presence by worshiping him and thanking him for all the ways he has already protected you. Then picture yourself resting safely in the shadow of the Most High.

Promises in Scripture

> *Those who live in the shelter of the Most High*
> *will find rest in the shadow of the Almighty. . . .*

If you make the LORD your refuge,
  if you make the Most High your shelter,
no evil will conquer you;
  no plague will come near your home.
For he will order his angels
  to protect you wherever you go.
They will hold you up with their hands
  so you won't even hurt your foot on a stone.

PSALM 91:1, 9-12

I cry out to God Most High,
  to God who will fulfill his purpose for me.
He will send help from heaven to rescue me,
  disgracing those who hound me.

My God will send forth his unfailing love and
  faithfulness.

PSALM 57:2-3

Continued Prayer and Praise

Genesis 1
Psalm 108:3-5
Isaiah 40:22
Mark 13:31
John 1:1, 51
Romans 11:33-36
1 Timothy 6:16
Jude 1:25

ACKNOWLEDGMENTS

I am grateful to Ron Beers and Lisa Jackson at Tyndale House Publishers for enthusiastically supporting a book on the attributes of God. Special thanks to Stephanie Rische for her masterful editing of the text. Not only did Stephanie offer many helpful suggestions and improvements, but she also gave the invaluable gift of prayer and encouragement as I was writing the book and then working on final edits.

Jon Farrar provided crucial support when it came to titling the book and deciding on a design direction for the cover.

Thanks also to April Kimura-Anderson and her team for their work in marketing and promoting the book.

As always, my agent, Sealy Yates, has provided wise counsel, support, and helpful perspective throughout the process.

These acknowledgments would be incomplete were I not to mention A. W. Tozer, whose books on the attributes of God enriched my understanding of who God is. Even though he died in 1963, his books still speak eloquently of the goodness of God and are worthwhile reading for Christians today.

NOTES

A CRASH COURSE ON GOD

1. Dylan Stableford, "Deaf Man with New Hearing Aid Hears Music for the First Time, Asks, 'What I Should Listen to Next?'" *The Sideshow* (blog) Yahoo! News, August 9, 2012, posted on http://news.yahoo.com/blogs/sideshow/deaf-man -hears-music-first-time-143827917.html.
2. For this insight I am indebted to Adrian Crum at Haven Ministries.
3. A. W. Tozer, *The Attributes of God Volume 2* (Camp Hill, PA: WingSpread Publishers, 2001), 6.
4. Robert K. Massie, *Catherine the Great: Portrait of a Woman* (New York: Random House, 2011), 340.
5. A. W. Tozer, *The Knowledge of the Holy* (New York: HarperCollins, 1961), 78.
6. C. H. Spurgeon, *Spurgeon on the Attributes of God* (Tampa, FL: MacDonald Publishing Co.), 92.

CHAPTER 1: GOD CARES ABOUT YOU

1. John S. Dickerson, "The Decline of Evangelical America," *New York Times Sunday Review*, December 15, 2012, http://www.nytimes.com/2012/12/16/ opinion/sunday/the-decline-of-evangelical-america.html?pagewanted=all&_r=0.
2. C. S. Lewis, *Mere Christianity* (New York: HarperCollins, 1952), 63.

CHAPTER 2: GOD IS BETTER THAN YOU THINK

1. C. S. Lewis, *Mere Christianity* (New York: HarperCollins, 1952), 93.

CHAPTER 3: GOD IS BIGGER THAN YOU THINK

1. A. W. Tozer, *The Attributes of God Volume 1* (Camp Hill, PA: WingSpread Publishers, 1997), 7.
2. Blaise Pascal, *Pensées* (New York: Penguin Books, 1995), 45.

3. Judith Martin, *Miss Manners' Guide to Excruciatingly Correct Behavior, Freshly Updated* (New York: W. W. Norton & Company, Inc., 2005), 692.
4. The covenant name for God is formed by the four Hebrew consonants *YHWH*, also known as the tetragrammaton. Though the exact pronunciation is uncertain, most scholars think the name is pronounced *Yahweh* (yah-WEH).
5. Adapted from Romans 8:38-39.

CHAPTER 4: GOD IS NOT MOODY
1. Written and composed by Joseph Brackett in 1848.

CHAPTER 5: GOD IS NOT WEAK
1. C. S. Lewis, *The Problem of Pain* (New York: HarperCollins, 2001), 18.

CHAPTER 6: GOD IS CLOSE TO EVERYWHERE
1. A. W. Tozer, *The Attributes of God Volume 1* (Camp Hill, PA: WingSpread Publishers, 1997), 118.
2. Ibid., 119.
3. Jerry Sittser, *The Will of God as a Way of Life* (Grand Rapids, MI: Zondervan, 2004), 25–26.
4. Charles G. Finney, *The Autobiography of Charles G. Finney*, condensed and edited by Helen Wessel (Minneapolis: Bethany House Publishers, 1977), 21–22.

CHAPTER 8: GOD IS NEVER FRUSTRATED
1. C. H. Spurgeon, *Spurgeon on the Attributes of God* (Tampa, FL: MacDonald Publishing Co.), 64.
2. William D. Mounce, ed., *Mounce's Complete Expository Dictionary of Old and New Testament Words* (Grand Rapids, MI: Zondervan, 2006), 501.

CHAPTER 9: GOD ALWAYS KNOWS WHAT TO DO
1. A. W. Tozer, *The Knowledge of the Holy* (New York: HarperCollins, 1961), 60.
2. A. W. Tozer, *The Attributes of God Volume 2* (Camp Hill, PA: WingSpread Publishers, 2001), 136.

CHAPTER 10: GOD HAS NO LIMITS
1. A. W. Tozer, *The Attributes of God Volume 1* (Camp Hill, PA: WingSpread Publishers, 1997), 5–6.
2. J. R. R. Tolkien, *The Hobbit* (New York: Random House, 1996), 1.
3. Anne Graham Lotz, quoted in Jeremy Weber, "Billy Graham's Daughter Asks for 'Urgent Prayer': 'We're in the Fight of Our Lives,'" ChristianityToday.com, http://blog.christianitytoday.com/ctliveblog/archives/2012/12/billy-graham-daughter-asks-for-urgent-prayer-anne-graham-lotz.html.
4. C. S. Lewis, *The Screwtape Letters* (San Francisco: HarperCollins, 1942), 78.

CHAPTER 11: GOD IS A LOVER

1. Mark Galli, *A Great and Terrible Love: A Spiritual Journey into the Attributes of God* (Grand Rapids, MI: Baker Books, 2009), 115.
2. George H. Morrison, "The Jealousy of God," in *Classic Sermons on the Attributes of God*, comp. Warren W. Wiersbe (Grand Rapids, MI: Kregel Publications, 1989), 36.

CHAPTER 12: GOD IS ALWAYS FAIR

1. Addison H. Leitch, "Righteousness," in *Zondervan Pictorial Encyclopedia of the Bible*, ed. Merrill C. Tenney (Grand Rapids, MI: Zondervan, 1975), 5:115.
2. Ibid., 5:108.
3. Tim Stafford, "Imperfect Instrument: World Vision's Founder Led a Tragic and Inspiring Life," *Christianity Today*, February 24, 2005, http://www.christianitytoday .com/ct/2005/march/19.56.html.
4. C. H. Spurgeon, *Spurgeon on the Attributes of God* (Tampa, FL: MacDonald Publishing Co.), 66–67.
5. Ibid.

CHAPTER 13: GOD LEANS TOWARD COMPASSION

1. Abraham J. Heschel, *The Prophets* (New York: Harper Perennial, 1962), 365.
2. Ibid.
3. Mary McCarty, "Why Did Story of Collapsed Runner Inspire People Worldwide?" *Dayton Daily News*, June 9, 2012, http://www.daytondailynews.com/news/lifestyles /why-did-story-of-collapsed-runner-inspire-people-1/nPR7x/.
4. Jim Cymbala, *Breakthrough Prayer* (Grand Rapids, MI: Zondervan, 2003), 69.
5. Henry Ward Beecher, "The God of Comfort" in *Classic Sermons on the Attributes of God*, comp. by Warren W. Wiersbe (Grand Rapids, MI: Kregel Publications, 1989), 91–92.

CHAPTER 15: GOD IS BETTER THAN ANYONE YOU KNOW

1. Annie Dillard, *Teaching a Stone to Talk* (New York: HarperCollins, 1982), 52.
2. A. W. Tozer, *The Knowledge of the Holy* (New York: HarperCollins, 1961), 1.
3. John Stott, *The Beatitudes: Developing Spiritual Character* (Downers Grove, IL: InterVarsity Press, 1998), 5.

CHAPTER 16: GOD IS AN ARTIST

1. John Merigian, http://www.johnmerigian.com.
2. Thomas L. Friedman, "Pass the Books. Hold the Oil.," *New York Times*, March 10, 2012, SR1, http://www.nytimes.com/2012/03/11/opinion/sunday/friedman-pass -the-books-hold-the-oil.html.
3. Ibid.

CHAPTER 17: GOD IS ABOVE IT ALL

1. Chris Wickham, "A Diamond Bigger than Earth?" cnews, October 21, 2012, http://cnews.canoe.ca/CNEWS/Science/2012/10/21/20297606.html.
2. Clara Moskowitz, "Space Diamond, Larger than Earth, Spotted by Astronomers," NBCNEWS.com, October 11, 2012, http://www.nbcnews.com/id/49375536 /ns/technology_and_science-space/t/space-diamond-larger-earth-spotted -astronomers/#.UbDkOPmyDzg.
3. Gregory Titelman, *Random House Dictionary of Popular Proverbs and Sayings* (New York: Random House Reference, 1996).
4. Quoted by Leslie C. Allen in *The International Bible Commentary*, ed. F. F. Bruce (Grand Rapids, MI: Zondervan, 1986), 620.

ABOUT THE AUTHOR

ANN SPANGLER is an award-winning author, publishing her first book and bestseller in 1994. She has continued to author several bestselling books, including *The One Year Devotions for Women*, *Praying the Names of God*, *Praying the Names of Jesus*, and *Women of the Bible* (coauthored with Jean Syswerda). Together her books have sold millions of copies. Her sensitivity to the ever-changing spiritual and cultural climate in which we live has enabled her to address themes of profound interest to many readers. She and her two daughters live in Grand Rapids, Michigan.